WHICH WAY
IS HOME?

WHICH WAY IS HOME?

by
Leslie Williams

THOMAS NELSON PUBLISHERS
Nashville

Published in Nashville, Tennessee, by Thomas Nelson, Inc., Publishers
and distributed in Canada by Lawson Falle, Ltd., Cambridge, Ontario.

Printed in the United States of America.

Scripture quotations on page 52 are from the Revised Standard Version of the Bible, copyrighted 1946, 1952, © 1971, 1973.

Quotes from Paul Tournier's *A Place for You* on pages 55 and 56 are
from the translation by Edwin Hudson (New York: Harper & Row,
1968) pp. 14 and 39, respectively.

The prayer on page 65 is from the Episcopal Church's *The Book of
Common Prayer,* p. 124.

References are made on page 101 and following to Mel Krantzler's
Creative Divorce (New York: M. Evans and Co., 1973), p. 212 ff.

Scripture quotations on pages 127 and 128 are from the King James
Version of the Bible.

The first and last stanzas of the poem on pages 132 and 133 are by
Steve Gold. Used by permission.

The quote from Milton's *Paradise Lost* on page 140 is from *The Norton
Anthology of English Literature,* vol. 1, edited by M.H. Abrams (New
York: W.W. Norton and Co., 1968), p. 1043.

Library of Congress Catalog Card Number: 81-9500

ISBN: 0-8407-5790-5

FOR STOCKTON

CONTENTS

Prologue 11
I. Suspicions 15
II. Trial Separation 30
III. The Bad News 43
IV. Aftermath 61
V. Summer 86
VI. Readjustments 105
VII. Resolution 131
Epilogue 134

WHICH WAY
IS HOME?

PROLOGUE

Two years ago I had a vivid dream. Our family was back together again, driving in our old blue station wagon "Bessie." We were on vacation somewhere with tall trees lined up like huge soldiers along the road.

My father was driving and my mother directed him from a map that looked like the Candyland board. Soon he turned off on a side road for no reason at all, and my mother became upset because we were late for something. My two sisters and I sat in the back seat biting our lips, because we didn't want our parents to get into a fight. Sure enough, though, they started throwing wadded Kleenex at each other and shouting.

About that time, the car turned into a cage on a Ferris wheel, and carnival music blared at us from all sides. While the Ferris wheel moved slowly up around its circle, my parents started chunking rocks instead of Kleenex, and they tried to push each other out of the cage. My sisters and I screamed and tugged at them to keep them in their seats. Suddenly the cage came loose from the top of the Ferris wheel, plunging toward the ground. We all cried and screamed, but just before the cage hit the ground, I woke up.

I sat up in the dark and hugged my pillow, trembling. It had been over two years since my parents divorced, and I was still being victimized by these occasional nightmares. Most of the time, during the day anyway, I handled the situations that arose out of their divorce just fine; in fact, I considered myself basically "over" the experience.

However, as I sat huddled in the dark, I began to realize that because I was still having nightmares about the divorce, I was probably *not* over it yet. I began to suspect that, at some level, I still had things to work through.

I said a prayer in the dark, thanking God for His comfort in times like this. I also prayed for healing to take place at the deepest level of my mind and soul, that place inside my innermost being where the nightmares were born.

Soon after that dream, I decided to write this book. I thought it might be helpful for two reasons. One was to see if I could come to terms with my own problems and questions by expressing in words many of the feelings which still sat in my stomach like tangled skeins of yarn. The other reason was to share these feelings with other young adults who might have similar experiences.

One thing my sisters and I discovered as our family was breaking apart was that very little attention has been given to the "grown" children of a divorce. Some books have been written about the traumatic impact a divorce has on small children. But what about those of us in our late teens or early twenties? At the time of my parents' divorce, the age span of the children in our family was eighteen to twenty-four. In spite of the fact that we were all supposedly considered adults, the experience was shattering for us. I had just finished graduate school, and I felt at times as confused and lost as had I been a small child.

I also wanted to talk about the way Jesus Christ has worked in my life during the divorce and its aftermath. My personal faith has been greatly strengthened in the last several years. God has helped me jump many hurdles as I struggled to reconcile the pain of divorce with His everlasting love and forgiveness.

As I began writing this book, I ran into a problem. How could I deal honestly with my feelings without revealing too much of my parents' personal lives? I felt it was only fair to protect them, so I have changed the physical setting and the details of their differences. But I felt it was also important to deal up front with the issues facing children in this situation. So I wrote this book in the form of a diary of a typical college student whose parents go through a divorce. I give careful account of the emotions *I* faced and experienced, as well as relating other emotions and crises I feel are common in circumstances similar to my own. But I have not detailed my own parents' situation.

Now, as I write this, it has been four years since my parents divorced. Although occasionally I feel unsettled and sad about the divorce, I no longer have the bad dreams. All of us have gone on with the business of living, grateful for the healing power of God's grace.

I

SUSPICIONS

All day today I packed my books and clothes for school. It was difficult deciding whether or not to take my stuffed pig, Arabesque, who has sat on my bed since I was ten. But Mother convinced me I should. I thought it might be corny to have a stuffed pig in a freshman dorm, but she said she thought I'd be glad to have a little bit of home with me in a strange place.

Finally, about ten this evening, I was getting ready to take a shower when the phone rang. I could tell it was serious by the tone of both Mother's and Daddy's voices as they talked on two extensions. Turned out the Nelsons are getting divorced. Daddy and Mr. Nelson are cronies from way back. Mr. Nelson apparently has been keeping a girl friend in an apartment for about six months now and finally just up and walked out on Mrs. Nelson. When I came out of the shower, Mother and Daddy were talking in their room with the door

closed. It's weird around here all of a sudden.
Well . . . tomorrow is a big day.

❧❦❧

Breakfast was okay. I tried not to think that it
was my last meal at home before I left for college.
Cissy kept saying things like "Oh, good, after you
leave I can have all the bathroom drawers to myself." And Mother kept going over the checklist to
make sure I hadn't forgotten anything. Daddy was
very quiet. Then, when he was helping load the car,
he started talking about the Nelsons. Pretty soon it
was as if he couldn't stop talking about what had
happened to them. He kept commenting on it as a
"modern phenomenon," trying to analyze the
situation. It gave me the creeps.

Once Mother and I got in the car and waved
good-bye to everybody, I asked her if she and Daddy were getting along all right. She hesitated for a
minute, then told me that most people their age
start having marital problems, but that she and
Daddy were working very hard at getting through
middle age intact as a couple. I felt as if she had
slapped my face. Where on earth had I been the last
year? Why had I not noticed they were having
problems? I knew Daddy had been spending more
and more time at the office, but I guess I had been
so wrapped up in my senior year activities that I
hadn't noticed the way his absence had affected
Mother.

It was a quiet trip the rest of the way.

My roommate is a girl named Kathy whom I used to go to church camp with. She and her mom were already here when Mom and I arrived. I hadn't seen Kathy's mom in about two years, and it really struck me how nervous she was. She was like a chicken, pecking at Kathy and bobbing all around the room. To make matters worse, she had dyed her hair a bright red. I was ready to climb the walls after spending just an hour with her before she left—I don't know how Kathy stood being around her for any longer.

Mother and I both cried when we had to say good-bye. We promised to write often and to keep each other in our prayers. I will pray especially hard. I would just die if anything happened and my parents split up. I pray that God won't let something like that happen.

Since classes don't start until tomorrow, Kathy and I spent all day shopping for matching bedspreads and catching up on all that's happened during the last year. We're very excited about this year.

We stayed up talking until about two-thirty in the morning. Kathy told me that her mother is going through menopause and that it is affecting their family in strange ways. If Kathy's mother's nervousness is hard for Kathy to take, you can imagine what it's like for Kathy's father. She picks at him relentlessly—about his clothes, about how late he stays at the office, even about the way he slurps soup with his spoon. Then, she realizes what she is doing and cries.

I wonder if Mother is having problems with this. I suppose some women have more problems than others. Kathy told me about the mother of one of her friends. This lady, Mrs. Bonner, started having delusions that her husband was having affairs with several different women, and she thought her children were encouraging him. They would come home from school to find desk drawers, linen cabinets, closets emptied out all over the floor and their mom sobbing in the bedroom. She'd accuse them of taking their dad's rendezvous messages, then burning them. Their dad got the worst of it, but he just turned the other cheek because he knew he'd always been faithful to his wife. When she started accusing one of the neighbor's wives, however, he took her to a psychiatrist. The whole family was surprised when the doctor diagnosed her problem as hormonal and related to menopause.

I'm glad I have a long time before I'm faced with those problems. I feel as if I'm just now recovering from adolescence.

I do not understand what is happening to people my parents' age. Out of the thirty girls on my floor in the dorm, five have gotten phone calls or letters saying their parents are breaking up. It's scary. I'm getting paranoid about getting a letter from home.

I'm trying to figure out what happens to people. So many of the parents who are divorcing are in the age group forty-five to fifty-five. I wonder what it's like to be that age. Now, at my age, life is like a beautiful rosebud, exciting and full of promise. It seems as if there are so many opportunities and people to meet that the choices are endless. But I wonder what it will look like in twenty-five years. Maybe when you get to be forty-five or fifty, things don't look so rosy. Maybe you feel that you made some bad decisions when you were twenty, and maybe you have more regrets stacked up than blessings. Right now all the forked roads are out in front of me, waiting for me to choose the ones I want to take. I can't imagine what it feels like to look back, wishing I'd taken another road. Maybe part of the middle-age panic thing is the sudden feeling that the rewards of past decisions are crummy and the desperate attempt to change things before it's too late.

An ironic thing happened this morning when I went into the bathroom to wash my face. Here I've been wondering what it's like to grow older, and I looked in the mirror and discovered . . . a short, but definitely gray hair sticking up from my part. The first thing I did was to pluck it out as fast as I could. Then I stared at it under the light, a short wiry little sprig. There was no doubt about it. Everyone, whether aged two, twenty-two, or eighty-two, is caught up in the process of growing older, and I had run across my first physical reminder that I will not always be a spring chicken!

The big question is—how do you learn to age gracefully, accepting stage by stage all the things that happen to your body? Right now it's easy for me to say that it's the inner, spiritual things that matter. Then again, I have all my teeth, good eyesight, a full head of dark, healthy hair (with one exception), and I don't creak when I walk up the stairs. Even though I really do believe that spiritual things are more important than physical things, I'll bet it is terrifying to wake up one morning and realize that the largest part of your earthly life is gone. It must be hard to wave good-bye to all the old promises of life that you suddenly realize will never come true.

·◄░░░►·

Kathy and I were talking along these lines last night before we went to bed, and she said she'd heard it put this way: "Multiply twenty-five times two and you get fifty; multiply forty-five times two and you get ninety."

My political science teacher is a man who's about forty-five years old and married. He isn't ugly, by any means; however, he certainly is no Adonis. He also has a nondescript personality. But I've heard he's having a "thing" with his graduate assistant, who is a gorgeous blonde girl at least six inches taller than he is. I was shocked when I found out. All I could think about was *why?* Maybe she thinks he's glamorous or something. Maybe it's all part of male menopause for him, and he feels he has to prove that he's still young and attractive. I'll bet it's part of the frantic last-minute grab at recapturing youth.

I called home last night about 10:30, and Mother was there by herself. Daddy was still at his office, and Cissy was spending the night at a friend's. What upset me was that Mother had been crying. She said she felt old and ugly. After I hung up, I felt so bad for her. It didn't seem to matter that to other people she really looks young and beautiful; it was how she felt about herself. It was then I realized that Christians are not exempt from fears of getting old.

I mean, Mother knows full well that we don't have to worry about getting old and dying—Christ has made an eternal place for us. It's just that I've never seen her get so down in the dumps over something like this. When I was twelve and got burned on my face, she was the one who kept telling me that it's what's inside that matters, not what you look like. But I remember how miserable I was and how long it took me to understand that God loves me no matter what.

I have to admit that I was a little scared about coming to college. I had my own group of friends in high school, and I didn't know many people who would be here. I didn't know how well I would make friends. Now that I've been here a month and a half, I love it. Of course, I have a super roommate, which helps, but I have also had the chance to meet a lot of great people in my classes, and through others in the dorm. I can't imagine that I ever wanted to stay back in my home town! Just think of what I would have missed. I wonder if this is true of all the stages you go through in life. I wonder if parents are afraid of the next stage in their lives because it is unfamiliar to them.

I've been going out some with a guy named John Haskill. He is not going to be the love of my life, but he's a good friend. He's from here, and we go to church together sometimes. Well, last Sunday,

John's minister announced to the congregation that he had decided to leave the ministry. Out of the blue he said that he and his wife were divorcing and that he had made plans to move out of the state. John found out today that the minister is planning to marry a woman he has been seeing. John called me, stunned. He kept saying how much he had thought of the minister, how gifted he was at teaching the Bible. John had thought this man embodied all the Christian characteristics he admired the most. John had known him for a long time—the minister had confirmed John and his brother when they were eleven—and he had always seemed too committed, too sincere about his walk with Christ to let that kind of temptation make him stumble.

It seems that committing adultery is as common as brushing your teeth. You see it on TV, you see it all around you. People seem to think nothing about having affairs. All the magazines and books try to make those regular married couples who don't believe in adultery look like prudes or creatures from out of the Dark Ages. We're all supposed to be so "free and easy" these days—all the movies and TV ads imply that happiness lies in this kind of freedom.

I just don't swallow it. Oh, I don't think Queen Victoria had the right idea either, but I also don't believe that all the bed-hoppers these days feel completely guiltless, or "right" about it. I think that rules to the game still exist, whether people choose to play by them or not.

⊷❀⊶

Kathy is getting bad vibes from home. Her older brother wrote her and said that one of his friends saw her dad and another woman on an airplane together going to Washington, D.C.—on the weekend he had told everyone he had business in Chicago. When this involves your own parents or the parents of someone close to you, well, it's the difference between reading the statistics of car accidents in the paper and nursing your best friend through a broken leg after a wreck.

Kathy's parents are coming for homecoming this weekend, as they've planned to do since this summer. She has two days to get ready for the encounter. Her brother thinks her mom knows about the other lady.

⊷❀⊶

Kathy and I stayed up last night talking about the Christian aspect of adultery. I think that Christians have stronger feelings about it than most people because of Christ's teaching and the Ten Commandments. But even among Christians the attitudes vary. On one end are the people who think breaking the commandment against adultery is at least as bad as murdering someone. To them, it's a heinous crime, indulging the blackest part of our human nature. On the other end are those who think it's a "mere" sin of the flesh, a sin which can't begin to stack up to, say, pride. Kathy and I decided that most people struggle in between. They recognize that adultery is wrong and a source of evil, but at the same time they see that even strong Christians are capable of lusting outside of marriage.

Kathy is just wondering why her father couldn't be content with stopping there and dealing with it.

What a weekend. It was terrible even for me, and I'm not directly involved. Kathy's parents had decided beforehand to pretend that nothing was wrong. They didn't know that Kathy knew anything. So all Friday night everybody put on a big jovial act, as if things were just swell. They invited me out to dinner, and Kathy's dad carried on a robust conversation about everything under the sun. Kathy's mom just sat there; she wasn't nervous or shifting around—she was utterly numb.

Saturday afternoon, Kathy's mom said she had a headache and said she'd rather lie down while Kathy's father and the other couple they drove down with went to the game. Kathy took that as a signal that she needed to talk, so she said she didn't want to go either. I was glad I had a date for the game, so I wouldn't be hanging around.

Kathy's mother has come unglued. She is crushed, devastated about what has happened. Not only is her ego shattered, but she feels that any trust she and her husband had built up over the years has been wiped out. She doesn't know what to do. Kathy's father hasn't asked her mother for a divorce, but her mother knows how unhappy he is.

Kathy's mother's reaction is so bad that even the sight of Kathy's dad brings physical revulsion. But at the same time, she knows that if the marriage is to be held together at all she needs to forgive him and try to forget the whole thing. She knows that the success or failure of the marriage depends a great deal on her ability to forgive and let the wounds heal. She is afraid that even if she is able to forgive Kathy's dad, the relationship will suffer. Yes, life will go on, but not as before. Little walls will be kept up between them; and Kathy's mom is afraid that the easiness and understanding they used to have is gone forever.

Another aspect of it is that Kathy's mom doesn't know how Kathy's dad really feels. He has said he is sorry, but Kathy's mom can't figure out if he is sorry enough not to have another fling. She doesn't know his motives for having the affair in the first place. Was he looking for a way out of the marriage? Was he in some way trying to get attention from Kathy's mom? Does he want to come back and try to make things work with them, or did the affair simply burn itself out? Kathy's mom feels that, with Christ's help, she can forgive him and make the marriage work—but only if Kathy's dad also wants it to work and is willing to try.

Kathy was still awake when I came in at midnight. Her parents had left after the game, and she had gotten into her pajamas and just stared at the walls until I came in. I made her some tomato soup in my popcorn popper and sat with her until she dozed off.

Sunday I took her to John's church and told her about the minister. She wonders how the minister's children feel about him. Will they ever be able to understand why he left his wife and his calling for another woman? Kathy says she feels so helpless, like an onlooker watching her family house burn down. She also wonders if her father, before he got into the affair, had ever considered what the effects of it would be on everybody else in the family.

The art lab John and I attend was cancelled this afternoon, so we decided to drive across town to see an art exhibit that we are required to see before the end of the semester. On the way, he told me about his graduate dorm advisor. (Even though John's parents live in town, he decided to live in the dorm at least for a year, so he can have the experience of living away from home.) John and his dorm advisor, Sean, have gotten to be pretty good friends— both are interested in advertising—and John was telling Sean about his minister. As it turns out, Sean had a similar thing happen to his parents, only it was the other way around. Sean was a sophomore in high school, fifteen, when his mother started seeing an old college boy friend who had divorced his wife and moved back to town. Sean had figured out that his parents were having problems; he had overheard part of a conversation. His father had said, ". . . but I don't feel that way anymore, toward you or anybody else. It doesn't disgust me; I'm just not interested." His mother had responded, "Is there anything about me that doesn't bore you?" to which his father had replied, "Don't ask me that," and calmly walked out of the room, ignoring Sean who had just walked up to ask if he could use the car.

Sean found out about the affair when his mother decided to move into an apartment across town without telling her husband. One Saturday, his mother told Sean to stuff all his things into boxes and sacks and with no further explanation guided him out the door to the car. His dad was gone for the weekend. When they got to the new place, Sean demanded to know what was going on. He didn't want to know all the details, but he thought he deserved at least an explanation. So his mother told him.

His father was no longer interested in her as a woman, and she had been seeing an old boy friend. She also said that there would be no child custody suit filed along with the divorce. Sean's father had agreed, in spite of everything, to let Sean's mother have custody of him. Sean stood calmly by the door taking it all in, then he hitch-hiked back to his house, got on his motorcycle, and disappeared for about eight hours. He said he considered leaving home for good, but he got hungry so he came back.

The next few months, Sean was a hellion on wheels. He says now it was lucky that he took it all out on the pavement instead of getting into drugs. He couldn't have verbalized it then, but he resented his mother for ruining their home. He resented his father, who had seemed to lose his virility—and his interest in Sean—without a fight. Caught in between, he begrudged his mother's need to see the old boy friend and despised his father's lack of manhood. He never talked about it to anybody though, and when people asked him, he just shrugged his shoulders and said, "Yeah, my folks ripped the sheets, okay."

Then, about two years later, he was still wrestling with what had happened with his parents and trying to figure out what the whole macho/manhood thing meant for him. He was seventeen when he got a girl he was dating pregnant. To make a long story short, he married her, tried to support her as a mechanic (he had to drop out of high school), and after two years divorced her. Now Sean is twenty-six, a graduate student in advertising who seems to have come to grips with his problems. He adores his kid. But he told John that it took him this long to work through all the problems, and it's been no bed of roses. He said when something like that happens to your parents, you can either react without thinking, as he did, or you can let it ruin your life, or you can work at it and get things straight. It's up to you.

II

TRIAL SEPARATION

All seems to be quiet on the home front. Maybe too quiet. I keep asking Mother if everything is okay, and she always answers that they are getting along fine; that Daddy stays at work late a lot, but she is finding things to do to take her mind off being lonely. Cissy told me that the atmosphere is strained around the house when Daddy is there. There is lots of obvious small talk, followed by long silences, then short outbursts of fighting. Cissy said these outbursts remind her of quick thundershowers that come and go but don't clear the air. After one of these, either Mother or Daddy quickly leaves the room. I wonder what's really going on.

Kathy had an insight today that helped me. She is handling her parents' problems very well. I think I would be so upset if I were in her shoes that I couldn't think straight. She thinks her dad is going to file for divorce any day now. We were talking today, and she said she thought that her father's affair was not the result of careless or irresponsible behavior. She thought it was a last resort as an outlet for frustration and unhappiness that had been brewing inside him a long time. She thinks he sought out this woman, not for herself but as a person in whom he could shore up all his doubts and anxieties. She thinks the whole affair was not based on sex—that sex was only the arena where these underlying needs were played out.

Then after she came out with all these insights, she said, "Of course, I hate what he did to Mom. And I pray every day that I'll be able to forgive him. I can barely speak to him any more. I'm afraid that because of what he did, I'll never be able to really trust a man in a close relationship."

It seems to me that adultery spreads chaos and unhappiness to everybody involved. Even the people who are supposed to be enjoying themselves seem to be all torn apart by guilt and split loyalties. I suppose it's easy for us to judge harshly, though. In the last analysis, I have to agree with Kathy. She said that, after all, to commit adultery is to break one of God's commandments. Therefore, God, not her, has judged the matter. He has already spoken. And that, she said, was the hard part.

❊❊❊❊❊

I just called home and found out that Cissy has been accepted by the girl's school she wanted, and she's going to start in January! She has been toying around all fall with the decision of whether she wanted to finish high school at a boarding school, or stay at home the last year and a half. She told me privately that she really wants to leave because things are so uncomfortable at home. Each of the parents asks her opinion about things going on and then uses her opinion to back up his or her argument against the other parent. Cissy feels they have several big problems to work out between them, and they are using her as an excuse not to face the issues.

It scares me. What's going to happen when there is nobody at home for the folks to focus their attention on?

If we lived in the Middle East or the Orient, our parents would never be faced with an empty house. Instead of getting our own apartments after college, we'd simply marry and move back in with them. Wouldn't that be something—three or four generations living with each other. I can hear it now: all the women arguing over who is boss in the kitchen, the husbands complaining about who takes out the garbage, and a million little kids squealing and crying. What a rambunctious arrangement!

But I'll bet it would never be lonely. And I'll bet the divorce rate would be a lot lower; because one thing I noticed in the five cases of girls in my dorm whose parents are getting divorced is that all but one of the girls are last or only children. I figure the parents were either waiting until the last child left home, or they didn't know how to handle it when there were just the two of them again.

Well, Kathy's father filed last week. She flew home over the weekend to be with her mother. Kathy's father is very mixed up right now. He took off to South America for a month to be by himself and to look at a ranch he might buy in Argentina. Kathy's been so worried and upset herself these last few months, she's afraid she may not pass some of her classes this semester.

Kathy's father called her long distance from Buenos Aires tonight. Kathy wasn't sure why. The closest thing she could figure out was that it was intended as an apology or an explanation of things. He rambled on about what he was doing in South America and then he said, "Your mother and I didn't have anything to say to each other at the dinner table any more—I felt like the contract ran out. I wanted to tell you I'm sorry." After Kathy hung up, and after she quit crying, she said what he probably meant was that an unspoken agreement in the marriage had run out. He had talked along those lines before. The tacit arrangement was that he would provide Kathy's mother with the security of financial stability for the family, and Kathy's mother would provide him with the security of making a home and raising the children. This seems to be the unwritten code for lots of marriages. Somebody's called it, "As long as we both shall love."

Frankly, I'd think parents would be glad to get rid of us. No more teen-age rebellion, no more moodiness around the house. I know lots of people who've done just fine when the kids left. I guess it depends on how strong the marriage is in the first place.

⟶❊❊❊❊❊❊⟵

The boys' floor above us invited our floor up to their lounge to watch the Friday night late movie, *Dracula*. They provided the Cokes, and we brought popcorn. It was great. After the movie was over, we all sat around, laughing and talking; then we got into some pretty serious and deep discussions. There were about six or seven of us there at that point—everybody else had left.

Kathy and I discovered that the same thing had happened on the boys' floor as had happened on ours. Out of twenty-seven boys, six had parents who had either divorced in the last year or who were in the process of a divorce.

One guy named Don Davis told what had happened to his family. He was the youngest child, and when he was still in high school, his mom started looking ahead to what she called the "yawning empty years." She decided that being a lady of leisure would be excruciatingly boring after about one month. So she enrolled in law school, part-time at first, so she could still carpool and fix dinner and so forth. When Don left home last year, she finished her law degree and went to work as a tax attorney in a private law firm. She loved working, but Mr. Davis couldn't get over Don's leaving and he couldn't handle his wife's career. Don thinks he was threatened and lonely, but his dad wouldn't admit to either. So he started drinking too much at parties. Soon he couldn't get through the evenings at home without four or five drinks; then finally he started drinking before work and then all day long.

All through the summer Mr. Davis threatened and abused Mrs. Davis during his drunken fits. In July, she started going to a counselor, alone because Mr. Davis wouldn't go with her. He continually refused to admit he had a problem.

Finally, after a year and a half (Don is a junior this year), Mr. Davis wouldn't acknowledge her presence in the house or speak to her, either when he was drunk or when he was sober. So Mrs. Davis told him she was moving out until he went to A.A. or to a counselor. His answer was to file for divorce, claiming that she had become a lousy wife.

There was another guy there named Chad, who has a twin brother at another school. He said his parents had trouble, too, after he and his brother left. Chad's father had inherited the family hardware store when he was in his early thirties and the twins were little. He had struggled for fifteen years to turn it into a profitable business, and he had succeeded. From a nearly bankrupt operation, he turned the hardware store into a state-wide chain. (As it turns out, that's the hardware store where my father trades all the time.)

About the time that Chad and his brother were leaving for college, a large national company offered to buy Chad's father out. He accepted, and not only did the national company pay him well, but they made him a vice-president.

When the deal closed, after an autumn filled with business trips back and forth to New York and extensive, exhausting negotiations, he finally came back home and discovered that his wife was suffering from severe depression. She had no energy or desire to leave the house, and several days a week she stayed in bed. The twins tried to call her often and cheer her up, to no avail. Their dad promised her a trip to Europe, told her she could redecorate the living room, and tried to stay home more with her in the evenings when she was too tired to get out. When nothing worked, he insisted she have a complete physical (she passed all the examinations), he suggested counseling (she refused), and finally he urged her to look for something to do, either church work, volunteer work, or a job. He really hoped she would pick up with her teaching career, but all his and the twins' encouragement failed.

Finally, one of her friends signed her up for a modern dance course at the junior college and practically forced Chad's mother to go. To everyone's surprise, she loved it. She told Chad that she had never done anything as creative and fulfilling as dancing. She signed up again, and after that session her class was asked to give a dance interpretation of modern poetry at the auditorium as part of Arts Appreciation Week. Soon afterwards, she and some friends started a small group of expressionistic dancers who visited civic groups as part of a cultural enrichment program. The twins thought this was great, but their father was appalled. This wasn't the sort of career he'd had in mind for his wife. For her to flaunt herself in a leotard and scarves embarrassed him, and he considered it not only vaguely sinful but extremely undignified for the wife of a top executive.

Toward the middle of the summer, when Chad and his brother were at home, their father confronted her with his feelings. She became furious, saying that it was his idea in the first place for her to become involved in something. For the next months, their arguments over her dancing became more and more bitter, encompassing more and more areas of their marriage. All the issues they had brushed for years under the rug of compromise came out in raging disagreements. Chad said it was awful. He could hear them in their room shouting at each other until late in the night. In early October his mother filed for divorce.

I came back to the room about 3:30 in the morning and hugged Arabesque, my pig, in the dark. I get this strange feeling in the pit of my stomach

when I think of what might happen when Cissy
leaves after Christmas.

⟡⟡⟡

Thanksgiving vacation was horrible. I got in on
Wednesday night, and I didn't have time to do
much visiting with the parents. But Cissy and I
stayed up late talking in her room about what has
been going on all fall. Apparently Mother is so listless she doesn't do anything except needlepoint all
day long. Cissy even has to do the cooking and the
washing and ironing.

Daddy is gone every night, and when he is there,
his presence is only physical. Whenever Cissy is
around him he seems preoccupied. And our parents' relationship has really deteriorated, even
since she told me about their fighting. They hardly
even speak any more except to argue, and both are
so stubborn they won't go see a counselor. Cissy
can't wait to get away.

Thanksgiving Day was even more of a nightmare.
Mother felt too bad to cook, so Cissy and I made the
turkey and dressing while Daddy watched the
games on TV. Then we had dinner, and afterwards
our next-door neighbors came over for dessert.
Most of the conversation was about how I liked
college, fortunately, because the atmosphere was
so tense that I was afraid things would explode in
front of our guests if we got on a topic closer to
home.

When I got back to school Sunday night, it was

no surprise to get a phone call from Mother saying that she and Daddy have agreed to a trial separation until Christmas.

Kathy and I are quite a pair. Her Thanksgiving, if you can believe it, was even worse than mine. Her mother cried the whole time and fussed at her for having cut her hair.

How am I supposed to make good grades when I am so anxious about my parents? On top of everything else, John Haskill has decided he's fallen in love with a girl over in his dorm, and so he never calls me anymore. I never had a crush on him, but I miss his friendship.

I wonder what God thinks about all this separation business. I know I should trust in His will for our lives, but I can't see how He can allow my parents to get a divorce. They are both Christians, and they are both good people. I don't understand, I just don't understand. If they get a divorce, does that mean that God has abandoned us?

Here I am worrying my head off that my parents will not be able to work out their problems, even after a separation, and I ran into a woman today in my small group at the adult Sunday school who was actually *relieved* when her parents got divorced. My parents had rocked along just fine for twenty-five years, then zappo—middle age hit like a thunderstorm, bringing with it all these mysterious problems. Cissy and I are hoping and praying that these problems can be resolved.

Sandi's experience was just the opposite. I guess I was never aware of those kids whose parents fought violently all the time. Sandi said she never knew when one parent would leave in a huff during the night. She grew up living in continual fear of abandonment, and after her parents got divorced, life seemed more peaceful and stable in comparison.

Sandi remembered one incident, one of many, she said, when her parents had been shouting at each other in their bedroom. Her father came out with his suitcase in one hand and a Kleenex in the other. His face bled where Sandi's mother had slapped him, cutting the skin with her ring. Sandi had been playing dolls in the living room, but when she saw her father, she ran to him and clung to his knees as he tried to leave the house. He had to push her away to get out the door.

Sandi's parents finally divorced when Sandi was twenty, her sister was seventeen, and her brother was twenty-two. All three of them were relieved when their parents separated, because all three had been affected by the hostility they'd grown up with.

The year before, Sandi's little sister had dropped out of high school and had gone to California during the hippie movement. She married a drug pusher and had a baby in a commune. Finally he left her, and she and her baby wandered around California until after her parents divorced. Then she went back to her father's house, where he put them up and arranged for her to see a good psychiatrist. Now she is happily married, but Sandi says that it cost her dad a bundle for four years of her therapy, plus all the regrets he has about the way he brought up the kids.

Sandi's brother is thirty-six and still unmarried. He told Sandi that he still can't express love in a close relationship. Because he was the oldest, he feels in some way responsible for the discord at home. Everyone's tried to assure him, of course, that he wasn't responsible; but now, years later, he never quite trusts anyone, especially women, long enough to open himself to intimacy with them. Sandi says he jumps from relationship to relationship, and—this is the ironic part—he usually ends each one with a violent argument. It's the only pattern he knows.

Sandi said she has a good marriage, but she went through several unstable stages during her teens and early twenties. She says the thing that saved her in the long run was her fear of getting involved with anyone she didn't trust. When she was a young teen-ager, she didn't date at all. She poured herself into her studies and devoted her efforts at home mediating between her parents.

She escaped into religion, believing that she was a martyr for Christ. She carried this idea of martyrdom into everything she did. She didn't have time for dating or fun. She thought self-denial was the essence of Christianity, plus she thought that if she worked hard enough at being the exemplary child, her parents would stop fighting.

This didn't work, of course, and when her parents split up, she felt at first very cynical about Christianity. Since she was now free of all the burdens she had taken on herself, she abandoned all her former attitudes and indulged herself by doing only what she wanted to do. Her grades hit rock bottom, she stayed out late night after night, and she took off overnight whenever she felt like it without telling anyone where she was going.

Eventually she realized this behavior was a bit extreme. She figured out that Christianity meant more than martyrdom. God had given her a life of her own to live, and He had plans for her particular gifts and talents to blossom. But she had to be responsible for herself and for what she did with her life.

I guess there's no easy answer. If parents fight all the time, it makes the children insecure and unhappy and makes them wish the parents would split up so each could find happiness somewhere else. On the other hand, it's bad if the parents get a divorce before they give themselves the chance to work things out.

III

THE BAD NEWS

I have managed to get all my Christmas shopping done before finals start. Except for one present. I have been going back and forth about whether to get my parents the backgammon set I saw. Daddy will be home for Christmas, but I don't know whether to get them separate gifts or the backgammon set together. Last year this wouldn't have been a problem.

❖❖❖

I think I did okay on all but one of my finals. Art was a breeze, but I'll be lucky to pass political science. The last two weeks, I've had a hard time sleeping. I keep waking up in the middle of the night. I sit up in the bed and find myself groping around in the dark. I am disturbed inside; I'm looking for something important, and I don't know what it is.

My dreams are not comforting. They aren't

nightmares with werewolves or frightening people in them, but they're filled with situations that don't resolve, or plans that fall through, or frustrating, unhappy things—strings of events that I can't remember when I wake up. I'm always exhausted in the mornings and usually very sad.

It is Christmas night, and Cissy and I are upstairs in her room. She is writing her thank-you notes already. She's always been more organized than I am.

Christmas this year was so poignant. Everything happened right on schedule, as it had all our lives, but every step of the way there was a feeling that "this might be the last time." We went to the family service at church after having a goose which Cissy and I cooked. We used the traditional Christmas dishes, and everyone agreed that it was the best goose ever. (We say that every year.)

Christmas morning, we all put on our robes and came downstairs to open our presents. The ritual made me so sad I could barely go through with it without crying. Daddy said the prayer, as he always does, and we recorded the whole proceedings on tape, just as we've done for years. Only this time—although nobody said anything—we felt we were recording for the last time. Therefore, it was important to be lighthearted and funny when we really felt rotten.

Anyway, the gifts we gave each other showed

what a bad state our family is in. Daddy gave us money, more than he's ever given us. I wondered why on earth he had given us so much—it made me feel as if he expected something in return. In a moment of high optimism I had bought the backgammon set for both parents. However, as soon as they opened it I regretted the decision, feeling like I had probably given them one more thing to fight over during the property settlement. Mother gave Daddy a new gold coin for the collection he sold six months ago without telling her; and Daddy gave Mother a beautiful robe and nightgown set made out of Qiana, which he had forgotten she was allergic to.

Cissy and I have spent the last week or so trying to talk with each of our parents. We just can't stand by and watch their marriage break up without doing anything. It's almost impossible to talk to Daddy, because he's not used to putting his feelings into words. The most we can figure out is that he's unhappy with himself, restless, and bored.

I can sit here and write this without sounding emotional, but during a short discussion I had with him, I got very upset. He doesn't seem to want to try to make the marriage work—he expects things to work out by themselves.

I'm afraid talking to Daddy isn't doing either him or me any good. For some reason, I understand Mother's helplessness better. No matter what she does, Daddy doesn't seem to be interested in her any more, so she has become listless. On the other hand, Cissy can talk with Daddy better than Mother. She feels it's Mother's fault that she hasn't made herself more interesting to Daddy. She says it's no wonder Daddy isn't trying.

It's all a big mess.

Cissy packed yesterday, and today she rode the train back with me. Her school is across town from the university, and she has a roommate who is also starting midyear. I took her to her dorm and helped her move in. It will be nice to have her close by. We've gotten through the stage where we used to fight, and we've become closer than ever in the last year or so.

Friday night the phone call came.

I was getting ready for a party, and I sat on the edge of the bed quite calmly while Mother told me that Daddy had spent the afternoon moving out for good. She seemed very calm herself, actually. After I hung up, I finished getting ready and met my date. About halfway through the party, it hit me. I was standing over a big bowl of potato chips and onion dip when the reality of it finally sank in. I started crying and couldn't stop. My date had to take me home.

Fortunately, Kathy was there. I called Cissy, and she came over. The three of us sat around and talked about how horrible it was. I felt as if I had been hit over the head with a two-by-four, in spite of the fact that I had known it was coming.

What is Mother going to do? This can't be happening to our family. I just can't believe it. Cissy and I are too shocked, too stunned, to think about what is going to happen.

❧❀❧

Cissy called this morning to say she doesn't think our parents will go through with it. I agree. I don't see how they can—not our family! Not our parents! Maybe they are using this as their last card to play—maybe they will get down to the wire, then call it off and get back together.

❧❀❧

More bad news. The proceedings are marching onward, and the community property is not easy to divide equally. So Mother either gets the house and very little income; or she can sell the house, move into a smaller place, and have some income for a while to get her started.

I'm outraged at that.

What on earth is Mother going to do? She has spent her lifetime raising us, like most of the women in her generation, and she has no marketable skills at all. She's never worked in her life, and how on earth is she going to find a job that will support her, when she's nearly fifty years old? It seems grossly unfair.

Cissy, of course, who always tends to side with Daddy, says she should have been developing herself all along. She says it won't hurt her to have to work for a living like the rest of the people in the world. I don't care. I still think it's unjust for her to be left in the lurch like that.

What if we *do* have to sell the house? I can't stand the thought of strangers living in the place where we made all our childhood memories.

Our parents built that house as our permanent home when I was six and Cissy was four. In the back yard is the swing where I fell off and broke my arm. I was kissed for the first time on our front porch. I used to daydream by the hour while looking out of the window in my room. So much is tied up in that place. I know I've moved away now—grown up and all that—but I will still feel like a refugee if we have to sell the house.

⁘⁙⁘⁙⁘

I feel as if God has drifted out of my life and disappeared behind the clouds. I know intellectually He's still there, but I don't feel His presence any more. I don't know how He can let this happen.

Maybe God doesn't just "let this happen." Maybe He's just as sad as I am over the whole thing—or more so. One thing I know—*I have to keep my trust*

*in Jesus Christ alive, because it's the only thing that's
going to get me through this nightmare.*

Cissy told me today that Mother definitely is
going to sell our house. She's already found a couple who wants to buy it. I feel so lost, so placeless,
rootless. Where is home, anyway?

I've been thinking a lot about this whole idea of
place and home. I get a lump in my throat when I
think of Dorothy Gale in the *Wizard of Oz* saying,
"There's no place like home, there's no place like
home." There is more to a home than a house; the
house represents the real home in our lives. Not
only is our house gone, with all its memories, but
worse than that, the "home" it represented is also
gone. The emotional network connecting the members of our family is gone. We were once like a giant
computer which ran on love and affirmation, and
now that computer has been torn apart, gutted.

Moreover, the "places," the roles, have all
changed. Mother isn't acting like a mother any
more. Sometimes she needs me to act like *her*
mother. All the old comfortable niches have disappeared. The same set-ups don't lead into the
punch lines any more. For instance, Mother has always had a hard time balancing her checkbook.

Everybody would laugh on occasions when we would get a call from the bank saying that Daddy's banker had put in extra money to cover for her. We all used to tease her and say, "Isn't that just like Mother." Well, now it's not funny any more. She's going to have to learn how to balance her checkbook, or she's going to get into trouble.

Another kind of place that's going to change is the "place" we had as a family in our hometown. All my life, I've been one of the Robinson clan, known by people in our church and in town who remembered my grandfather. Our family has been active in the church for three generations, and I was defined by who my family was and what we did in the community. I knew that this would change when I went away, but I always expected to be able to come home and step right back into our family's comfortable niche. Now Daddy is moving to another city, and things will never be the same as they were.

Kathy and I went to a meeting this morning for undeclared majors, which was essentially the entire freshman class. When I first came to college I thought I wanted to major in art or advertising, but now I just don't know. Kathy and I both left the meeting in a blue funk. This is a terrible time to try to decide on a major. We both feel totally lost; we've lost our bearings. We're confused about everything, not just school.

I feel as if I'm caught somewhere in that no-man's land between childhood and adulthood. I feel formless. Because I'm so desperate right now to find something I can hang on to, I'm afraid I will make some bad decisions, not just about what I want to do vocationally but about other things as well. So I shy away from deciding anything.

I'm afraid I'll wander for the rest of my life, from job to job, from relationship to relationship, looking for this "place" I have lost, scared to commit myself to anything.

Kathy has the opposite fear. She's afraid that she is going to grab onto things before she knows they're right for her. She has already declared her major as teaching, and she hasn't even really thought about it yet. She's clinging to her boy friend Bruce, whom she's only known for two months. I'm afraid she's going to get too serious with him too fast because she feels lost and he gives her temporary security.

I know what I need. I need to have patience and to stop myself from panicking at the thought of my loss of security. Yes, patience is what I need, patience to let each day roll by, patience to let my feelings of security grow strong again, patience to let my doubting faith become stronger. But I can't help it. I want security *now*, a home *now;* I want my faith strengthened *now*, my major decided *now*. I want to take a jet and be at my destination, where

I will once again feel secure and loved, *now*. Somebody once said that the journey was the destination, but right now I can't see it. I feel too lost.

Tonight I opened my Bible to the Psalms. I felt a great need to hear from God, to be reassured of His presence and love. As I read the Psalms, I was deeply moved by the ancient words of inspiration and comfort, and I copied down some of the verses here, so I can refer to them and learn some of them by heart.

> GOD *is our refuge and strength,*
> *a very present help in trouble.*
> *Therefore we will not fear though*
> *the earth should change,*
> *though the mountains shake in*
> *the heart of the sea. . . .*
> *The* LORD *of hosts is with us;*
> *the God of Jacob is our*
> *refuge (Ps. 46:1,2,11).*
>
> *For God alone my soul waits*
> *in silence;*
> *from him comes my salvation.*
> *He only is my rock and my salvation,*
> *my fortress; I shall not be greatly*
> *moved. . . .*
> *On God rests my deliverance and*
> *my honor;*
> *my mighty rock, my refuge is*
> *God (Ps. 62:1,2,7).*

After reading these and other verses, I felt quieted and more at peace. Through the ages, God has been the refuge of those who believe in Him; and now, during this frightening time in my life, I am reassured that He is my refuge, too.

I am not so lost any more.

Guess who called and asked me for a date? Chad Everson, whose father had the hardware stores. I met him when we all went upstairs to watch *Dracula*. He asked me out to dinner and to a movie.

He didn't know about my parents until we got in the car, and he was very nice. I found him easy to relate to. We had such a good talk during dinner that we decided to take a rain check on the movie, and we drove to a quiet, out-of-the-way café and sat and talked for the rest of the evening.

I told him the way I was feeling about being homeless and without a place, and he told me that he'd felt that way too. But with his brother, Mark, it was even worse. Mark, for some reason, had always been the homebody, the one who didn't even want to spend the night away. He had a hard time adjusting to being away from home his first year in college. But when his parents split up and his mother moved away, Mark went crazy. He spent the first three months getting high by himself in his dorm room or getting raucously drunk at fraternity parties. He said he felt as if all his bridges had been burned behind him and it didn't matter what he did, since he had no place ahead of him and he couldn't look back.

Finally, he started going to a counselor, someone professional to talk things over with. Chad said that was the smartest thing Mark ever did. The counselor gave him good advice, and Chad said that he, too, learned some things from what Mark told him. The counselor said that, yes, he had lost his "home"—his house, his sense of family, his place as a family member in the community. The first step toward healing was learning to accept that *things would never be the same again.* Mark had to find a new home. If he couldn't feel at home with either parent, then he had to find a home within himself. So wherever Mark went became home. His dorm room was his home, his car was his home. He carried home around with him.

Chad told me that he took this philosophy to heart himself, but he carried it one step further. He explained that he was a Christian, and he realized that Christ and His church are "home," our spiritual home. After working through some doubts he'd had about Christianity, he'd come to realize that we do not need to be tied to a place or to a set of circumstances to find our home in Him.

Chad gave me a lot to think about. I really liked him, right from the start. I like it that he's a Christian. When he brought me back to the dorm, he asked me out again to see the movie we had missed. I'm already excited at the thought of seeing him again.

I think of my life as taking place in a large house with many rooms. I was born in the basement and grew up in the rooms on the first floor. Then, just as I was ascending the stairs to go to the second floor, or to the next stage in my life, someone turned off all the lights and boarded up all the doorways to the ground floor. I know I can never go back, even to visit, and I am caught here on the staircase between floors.

When the lights first went out, I groped around, miserable in the dark, trying to get back downstairs. But now I realize that I am stuck here on the stairway—for a while, anyway—and I had better start making this place my home, even though it is a transition and not a plateau. The astonishing thing is that God has not left me in utter darkness, as I at first thought He had. One by one candles are being lit here and there around the house.

When Chad picked me up the other night for our second date, he brought a book for me to read, called *A Place for You* by Paul Tournier. He's so perceptive! Normally when people recommend books they are not what I need at the moment; but I can't believe how good this one is and how exactly right it is for what I'm going through.

The chapter on "Biblical Perspectives" is especially good. A couple of things the author says relate particularly well to the feeling of homelessness.

First, he describes man's first place on earth, a place God created for us, harmonious, beautiful, a place of perfection—the Garden of Eden. But everybody knows what happened to us and to the perfect garden. It stopped being a paradise and became a place of fear when Adam and Eve disobeyed God. Man was expelled from his place. "And so," says Tournier, "we see man committed to his life of endless wandering." This made me see that, as a child of divorce, I'm not exactly the first person to lose my place in life. It's our inheritance to wander, and the Bible is filled with homeless people.

Tournier talks about one of the most common places in which God's people wander—the desert. When I read that, I immediately thought of our family's trip to the Holy Land and our journey by bus from the Sea of Galilee to the Dead Sea and on to Jerusalem. I have never been to a place so hot, so desolate, so barren, where the human body, without water, will dry up and die in a matter of hours. I can appreciate the powerful imagery of a "desert experience." Tournier says, "The desert is deprivation and poverty, the place where man can rely on no security whether material or spiritual, but only on God."

So I guess an experience in the desert is an experience under horrible conditions. In spite of them, however, it can bring fruitful inspiration and a stronger faith. Look at all the people in the Bible who spent time in the desert to meditate and renew their spiritual lives—John the Baptist, Paul, Moses, and Jesus Himself. I suppose that we can consider our lack of place as a place itself—a desert.

※※※※

We had a surprisingly warm day today for February, and Chad called with an invitation to play some tennis. That's another thing we have in common: We both played on our high school tennis teams. Anyway, walking back to the dorm he asked me how I liked the book. Of course, that started a big discussion, and he came up with an insight I had never considered concerning placelessness.

"Look at Christ's life," he said. "Though God picked a specific time and place for His Son to be born, Jesus' later life and ministry was spent placeless, as He travelled from town to town. He was stoned out of Nazareth, His hometown, and He never had a geographical spot like a house that He could call His home. He was even buried in someone else's place. As for personal belongings, He had His clothes and shoes, and that's all. He didn't need familiar things around to create a place for Himself. He had His place not in any earthly location or circumstances, but in His Father."

I asked Chad if it had been easy for him to make the jump and give over to the Lord such a deep and fundamental thing as the need for security of place. He said it was terribly hard; that often still he feels lost and anxious. The difference is that, before, he always felt as if his little boat was going to capsize, whereas now he knows he has an anchor when the storms start whipping up the waves.

❊❊❊❊

Kathy is going through an odd stage. When her folks first broke up, she seemed so level-headed. But now she's very heavy with Bruce. This guy smokes dope and doesn't treat her well. She's been staying out all night a lot, and she pretends that everything is fine. All she'll talk about is how wonderful Bruce is and how much in love with him she is.

I'm worried about her.

❊❊❊❊

Everything's happened so fast I can't believe it. Spring break is next week, the first week of March, and it happens to be Cissy's spring break, too. We are going home together. I say "home" so glibly. We are going back to help Mother move out of the house into an apartment. On Friday of next week, the divorce will be final. I hope we will have her moved by then. This is one vacation I am not looking forward to.

Daddy has already moved. He bought a small condominium in another town, and according to Cissy, who got special permission to fly out there two weekends ago, it's all fixed up already. I just couldn't bear to go visit him yet. I couldn't face walking into a strange place, "Daddy's house," and seeing the things we grew up with in an unfamiliar setting.

When Cissy and I walked into our old house this morning, it was like a bad dream. Half the furniture was gone, all the pictures were off the walls, and mother had started boxing the knickknacks, which were in a pile in the center of the room. Daddy had taken all the bedroom furniture out of Cissy's room, so Cissy put her bags in my room where she was going to spend the night. We ate Kentucky fried chicken sitting on the den floor (Daddy had taken the kitchen table) and packed dishes and books until about midnight.

The day after we got home, Saturday, the movers arrived; and while they hauled off the big pieces, we finished packing the odds and ends. That night we stayed at Mother's new apartment, and the next day, after church, we went back to the house to clean up. We finished about seven o'clock and took one last look around the house to make sure we didn't forget anything.

Well, that did us all in. By the time we locked the front door, all three of us were crying our eyes out. We stood there on the front porch in the dark and held each other. Then we got in the car and drove away.

We've spent the rest of this week helping Mother get settled in her new place.

Today the divorce was final.

Since Daddy had filed, Mother didn't have to go to the courthouse. I was glad, because she is having a hard time getting over the fact that he actually went ahead with the divorce. She had not been happy in the marriage either, but she felt very strongly that divorce was not the answer. I'm afraid it would have been even worse for her if she'd had to go to the courthouse.

As it was, we got up fairly early, fixed breakfast, and sat around the breakfast room feeling sorry for ourselves. Finally, Cissy said, "I can tell it will be flooded around here by noon if we don't do something. I'm going to the movies, if anyone wants to join me."

At first Mother said no, that she didn't have the energy to do anything. But we convinced her to get up, take a bath, get dressed, and go with us.

So we went to see a double-feature matinee, which didn't really ease the pain but at least took our minds off it for a little while.

It's just going to take time. Lots of time.

IV

AFTERMATH

When I got back to school, Kathy was there. Bruce wasn't back yet. She asked how things went, and I told her about all that had happened. We went out for supper because the dorm kitchens weren't open yet and then came back and went to sleep.

The next few days things rocked along pretty smoothly, and I was beginning to think (with relief) that the bad part was over. Then an unexpected thing happened. I was sitting at my desk reading a short story for my English class, and the radio began to play "Send in the Clowns" by Judy Collins. It reminded me of last Christmas, when Cissy played that album over and over. I was suddenly furious and leaned over and threw the radio on the bed.

This volcano of anger! Where does it come from? This is shocking. I didn't know I had so much hostility inside me. Now that I start thinking about it, I realize I am mad because our family has broken up. I am angry because our parents couldn't work out their problems, angry because I am unhappy and miserable on account of something that isn't my fault. I am just mad as hell.

Since it was virtually impossible for me to keep studying this afternoon, I grabbed my tennis racket and balls and went out to hit against the backboard. I have a feeling my backhand will be greatly improved before this is all over.

❖❖❖❖

Chad came back this week. He took two weeks for spring break because he and Mark and their father went to Colorado skiing. It was the only time they will have with their father all year long.

❖❖❖❖

I got a letter from Roberta, a girl who played on the tennis team with me in high school. I think we are going to work together this summer, teaching at the tennis clinic. I ran into her during spring break and then wrote her when I got back to school.

I told her about the incident with the radio. When we were in high school, her parents divorced. At the time, she was the only one on the team whose parents weren't together. She had confided things to me then, although I realize now how little help I must have been. I couldn't possibly have understood what she was going through.

Anyway, she wrote me this letter:

Was I angry? I stayed mad for about a year. Mad at everybody who crossed my path. At first the victim was mostly Dad. As you know, he left Mom right after he'd been promoted to a bigwig position in the company. And even before it was final, he started dating these society babes who ooed and gooed over him until he started strutting like a peacock. What really killed me was that he left Mom before she'd had time to recover from her hysterectomy. Having a hysterectomy is debilitating enough without having your husband walk off, leaving you feeling like an old battered kite stuck in a tree. Every time I saw Dad I wanted to sock him in the face.

Mom, though, also had her turn as the victim of my anger. I expected her to take it hard, but I expected her at least to try and get over it. But no. She stayed in bed for six months, without calling her friends to do stuff, or getting out of the house except for church every once in a while. I coddled, I cooed, I pled with her to try to get her life going again. All she said was, "My life is over. I'm worthless. I might as well die."

Finally I blew up at her and told her she could ruin her life if she wanted to, but I was sick and tired of watching her waste her gifts and talents. And you know, after that she started going out some.

I guess I'm not the only one who gets angry.

The nights are still bad. I'm still having bad dreams, and I wake up sometimes with my fists

clenched and my heart pounding. I simply do not
know how to handle this anger, this unfocused
stream of emotion. How do you handle being angry
at a "situation"? You can't talk to a situation, or hit
it, or get back at it, or change it in any way.

Instead of letting my anger and frustration con-
sume me, I'm having to learn to lie back down in
bed and ask the Lord to help me accept the divorce.
I can only pray that night by night, flare-up by
flare-up, my anger will gradually settle into an
emotion I can handle.

It occurred to me today that anger is a selfish
beast. Although my anger is directed at people or
things outside myself, it shoots up from my own
deep hurt. Some of this anger is righteous anger
over what I think is the unfairness of it all. But my
anger is excessive and more self-centered than that.
I want to scream, *"I hurt!"* from every pore, until
I've lost sight of the reason I hurt and can think
only of the hurt itself.

I can already see a crucial effect of staying angry:
excessive, consuming anger doesn't change anything that has already happened. It makes the present miserable, and it destroys future chances for
growth and healing to take place. By indulging myself in anger, I am not only cutting myself off from
God, the source of love and healing, but I am stunt-
ing my own Christian growth because of a past I
can do nothing about. I know I must overcome this.
It's so futile to be angry. More than anything, I
don't want my anger to turn into bitterness—bit-

terness eats at you, like rust, from the inside out.

❦

Mother seems to be holding her own. She is finally going for counseling to a man at church who is supposed to be an expert at working with recently divorced persons. A nice man has asked her out, although at this point she isn't interested in dating. She is thinking of getting a job next fall, but she doesn't know yet what she wants to do.

Daddy has a girl friend. It sounds so weird to say these things. I'm so used to thinking of my parents as a unit, and it's hard to imagine either of them going out on a date with someone else. I guess I'll have to get used to the idea.

Cissy is making straight A's. She's always been smart, and now she is pouring herself into her school work. When I called her the other night, she seemed a little low. She hasn't made friends as quickly as she had thought she would. She and her roommate don't get along very well. She said that sometimes she gets pretty lonely in the night. Today I sent her my favorite prayer for the nighttime lonelies.

"Keep watch, dear Lord, with those who work, or watch, or weep this night and give your angels charge over those who sleep. Tend the sick, Lord Christ; give rest to the weary, bless the dying, soothe the suffering, pity the afflicted, shield the joyous; and all for your love's sake. Amen."

Kathy's done it now. I've hardly seen her at all since spring break, she's been with Bruce so much. Well, last night they went over the state line and eloped. I can't believe it. This afternoon she came back to the dorm room to pack up all her things. She says she isn't dropping out of school, but if she continues at the rate she's been going, she'll flunk out. I'm sure Bruce doesn't care if she finishes or not. I feel sorry for her because, when she came back to tell me, she didn't seem elated as a new bride should be. She seemed tired and sort of offhand about it all. And when she walked out the door with the last load, she got teary-eyed and said, "I'll miss you."

I wish her the best, I really do. However, I have big doubts about the whole undertaking.

And now I don't have a roommate.

Chad got some bad news from home yesterday. His father's had a heart attack. The doctor thinks he will recover, but he's going to need lots of rest and care the next few months. Since Chad's father doesn't have any close family except the twins, they have decided to alternate flying home on the weekends to be with him.

Chad loves his father very much. This really scared him. He's going to change his plans for the summer and go home to be with his father.

I hope his dad gets well quickly.

Even though my dorm advisor wasn't able to find me a new roommate, it looks as though I have an unwelcome one anyway—loneliness, the night creeper. Since Kathy has left and Chad's out of town a lot, I've been lonelier than I've ever been in my life.

I copied the prayer I sent Cissy and put it over my desk.

Loneliness is easy to recognize, but it's hard to overcome because it's the absence of something— love, fulfillment, meaningful activity, friendship.

The worst times for me are at night, from about nine until I go to bed, and on Sunday afternoons.

I have decided to set up for myself a whole new way of going about things. During my first semes- ter, people fell into my life without my having to do anything. Now that things have changed, and espe- cially since I am particularly susceptible to loneli- ness because of my parents' breakup, I am going to learn how to seek out people, how to reach out. I'm going to have to prod myself into action.

Last week I sat down and made a list of all the people I want to get to know better. Then I started calling until I found someone on the list who could go out with me. Before I called these people, I did some thinking and checking around about what we could do, what activities might be fun. I came up with lots of things—bicycling, tennis, roller skating, tossing a frisbee, taking a walk, the Sunday afternoon matinee, or, as a last resort, studying at the library. In fact, I called up Nicole, a girl in my history class, and we had a great time at the library. We sat across the table from two good-looking guys who also turned out to be in our history class. They took us out for Cokes afterward.

I figure that anything that interests me, such as outdoor concerts, art museums, sports, will interest somebody else, too; and it's much more fun to go to something with a friend.

The key, of course, is in being aggressive and not waiting around for somebody to call me. It's also hard not to get discouraged when I have to call several people. It's easy to think, "Oh, they don't like me." But after I called Nicole to study with me, she called me back at another time to play tennis.

❧❧❧❧❧

I have discovered more things going on around the campus, things I'd never paid much attention to before. There are all sorts of interesting activities—the cinema society, intramural sports of all kinds, madrigal singers, the art club.

The hardest part about going to a group meeting alone (because I am naturally shy) is forcing myself to stick around after the meeting for the social hour afterwards. Unless someone rushes up to me, I always tend to hang back from a group of people I don't know well, feeling awkward. So to get over the initial hump, I've decided to make myself go up to at least two people and start a conversation. Many times they seem to feel as awkward and shy as I do, and they're just waiting for someone else to break the ice. So far I've had good experiences, with the exception of one guy who was as friendly and warm as an iceberg and who made me feel unwelcome.

But he's been the only unfriendly one.

༺✦❈✦༻

I also decided to be a more active participant in the college group at the church. It's become essential for me to have a group of Christians to interact with, to share with, to worship with during this time. Even in the few weeks I've gone to the group, I've felt a difference in my life.

The first time I went, I knew only one person, Janice, a girl in one of my classes. (John Haskill used to attend, I guess, but he goes to his girl friend's church now.) Janice came right over when she saw me walk in and started introducing me to some of the others. That first meeting, I watched everyone talk and share with each other. They seemed to know each other very well, and I desperately wanted to be a part of their fellowship.

The next time I went, several people came up and talked with me, and I introduced myself to several more. During the small group session, I even felt "safe" enough to participate.

During the week, Janice and I went out to lunch after class, and we got to know each other better. She told me about her family. She was adopted as a baby by two loving Christians who have always had—and still have—a warm, caring relationship. She felt grateful, she said, for her family.

I told her about my family and my parents' divorce. Automatically, she reached across the table and touched my hand. "I'm so sorry," she said. "I know it must be hard. If you like, I'll pray for you."

I went back to the dorm feeling warmed and uplifted by our get-together.

The next week, we had a special service in the church before the college meeting. The service, a communion service, was a moving one. I felt that Christ opened my heart to His love and to the love of those people around me. Even though I was just beginning to know most of them, I felt the Holy Spirit moving among us, bringing us closer to each other. I was deeply grateful for the church, grateful that God has given us a community of believers who worship together and give each other strength in times of trouble.

There are still times late at night, or when everyone I call already has plans, when the loneliness won't go away. Sometimes I can read a book or work on the afghan I'm crotcheting for Cissy's birthday, and I don't feel as bad. If I can just get my mind off myself and onto something meaningful, it helps. When my interest is absorbed, I'm not sitting around moping and waiting for the feeling of loneliness to overwhelm me.

I suppose the most important thing I'm learning about loneliness is not to fear it. It isn't fatal. There are even times when I feel that loneliness brings me closer to a deeper part of myself.

I think I'm beginning to accept the fact that, yes, it sometimes comes and sits with me. It probably sits with everyone at one time or another. It is one of the shadow creatures which makes God's light seem ever brighter.

※※※

Today in my theology class we had a good discussion on guilt. It seems that actual guilt and feelings of guilt are two different things. Some people, according to the degree to which their consciences are developed, feel more guilty than others about the bad things they do. An example the teacher gave is this: Two boys steal hubcaps. One is pleased with himself—he didn't get caught, and now he has a new set of hubcaps. The other boy feels bad—the hubcaps aren't his, and he regrets having taken them. Both boys *are* guilty. Only one *feels* guilty. The teacher in my class then went on to talk about guilt, actual guilt and feelings of guilt, in relation to God's grace and the atonement.

I'm the type that feels guilty a lot. I don't know why—maybe it has to do with my upbringing. When I first came to college, I used to feel guilty if I went out for a Coke and pizza at night before I finished all my studying. I've eased up on myself a little bit in the last few months, but I'm still the type that feels guilty if I don't eat everything on my plate, guilty when I tell a white lie to spare some-one's feelings. And now, since I've had a lot of time to think about things lately, I've been haunted by feelings of guilt about my parents' divorce.

Oh I know, I know—all the divorce books say that the children of a divorce, especially small children, feel in some way responsible. I've read all about it: The children think that there's a direct correlation between imagined happenings and reality, that their thoughts have the magic power to come true. A small boy thinks Mommy left home because one time he got mad at Mommy and wished she would leave. Then suddenly, when Mommy really leaves, the little boy can't handle the enormous amount of guilt he feels. Or little kids think Daddy left be-cause they were bad children. So they work hard at being model children so Mommy and Daddy will get married again.

I can see through all that. I'm an adult (well, almost an adult); I'm not a small child. But all the clear thinking in the world doesn't stop this vague, lingering feeling of guilt—that I was in some way a contributor to my parents' unhappiness. I keep questioning myself over and over: Did I do every-thing I could to keep them together? No—I had my head in the sand my entire senior year and didn't even realize they were having problems.

Did I help push them apart by refusing sympathy

or by being sulky, uncooperative? Yes—the one time I tried to talk to Daddy, I only got mad at him. I couldn't understand what he was going through. And I was little help to Mother, either.

I couldn't even understand what was really going on between them.

These things bother me. I realize that, objectively, my behavior didn't have much to do with their decision to divorce. There was probably nothing I could have done to prevent it. Yet I can't seem to get rid of this after-ache, the feeling that there was something I could have done that would have made the difference.

Nicole and I have been doing a lot of things together lately. Turns out she is a good tennis player. She's been through a lot for her age; her family life has been very tumultuous. Her father, a native Frenchman, died when Nicole was ten. Then, when Nicole was fourteen, her mother remarried a man who not only squandered all of her mother's savings, but treated both Nicole and her mother harshly.

One night, after a year of being alternately ignored and shouted at, Nicole confronted him over something trivial. The confrontation led to an uproar that Nicole said was just awful. She ran back to her room, packed her belongings, and walked out the door. She told her mother she wasn't coming back until her stepfather was gone. After three

weeks, Nicole's mother picked her up at her grandfather's and took her home. She had filed for divorce.

All this came up when I told Nicole that I was
feeling guilty for not being able to save my parents'
marriage. Nicole said that working through her
guilt was the hardest thing she'd ever had to do.
After her mother picked her up at her grandfather's
and told her that she and her husband had filed for
divorce, Nicole felt terrible. She hadn't realized
what she was doing. Had she really forced her
mother to choose between her and her stepfather?
Had she really been the cause of the divorce?
Nicole said these thoughts were like arrows in her
side.

Fortunately, Nicole's mother talked with her for
a long time, and she assured her that her leaving
had only been the last straw. She said they'd dis-
cussed divorce since the first part of their marriage,
when she realized they'd made a mistake. If they
hadn't been on the brink already, she wouldn't
have let Nicole's behavior make a decision she
hadn't already made herself. This made Nicole feel
a little better, but she said that it has taken her *six
years* to work through all the guilt she heaped on
herself ... and she still feels bad every once in a
while.

Chad was here this weekend. To make up for all
the time he has been gone, he put together an enor-

mous picnic lunch, and we spent all day Saturday out at the lake.

His father is doing much better; he's recovered faster than the doctors at first thought he would. They say he ought to be back out on the golf course in another six weeks. Chad has been going up there nearly every weekend. He says that never again will he take his dad for granted.

He asked if I'd seen Kathy. I told him that I had called several times, but had only talked to her twice. The first time she sounded all right, but the second time she was high or something and didn't make much sense. Since she lives across town and neither one of us has a car, it seems our paths never cross any more. It makes me sad. I told him that I miss her a lot but that I am learning how to get over being so lonely.

Then we started talking about the guilt problem I've had lately. I asked him if he ever went through anything like that. He said he had experienced the reverse. Although he was bothered by questions such as, "What more could I have done?," it was in a different sense. He felt that he had done everything in his power, to no avail. Therefore he had felt useless, inconsequential, and abandoned.

He had talked and talked with his mother and his father and had done everything he could to ease the communication between them. But they seemed to disregard everything he said, and as a result he felt that he was not very important to them. With his rational mind, he knew that his parents were divorcing each other and not him; yet at a deeper level, he felt they were leaving him, because for some reason he wasn't good enough.

He said he had to sit himself down and make himself accept the fact that kids' influence over their parents' decisions is, in the long run, negligible, that parents lead their own lives unaided by their children's advice on major matters. He said it was something of a shock for him to realize that his parents, especially his mother, didn't exist for the sole purpose of raising Mark and him, to realize that parents have their own lives to live. He said he had to turn his parents loose in his mind, to let them go, knowing that they made their decision to divorce all by themselves, in spite of anything he did or could have done.

Chad made me see that my feelings of guilt had relatively little basis in fact. They were giant weeds thriving in the hothouse of my imagination. When I got back to my dorm room, I prayed for the Holy Spirit to help me pluck out the unqualified feelings. I knew I couldn't tell the difference between what I should feel guilty for and what I did feel guilty for, so I said a blanket prayer asking forgiveness for the actual guilt and the feelings of guilt.

After I closed the prayer, I remembered something Chad had said on our picnic. "Just remember, if God forgives you, who are you not to forgive yourself?"

I remember the first time our first-grade class had to give oral reports. We went in alphabetical order, and, being a little later in the alphabet, I felt confident that when my turn came I could do it easily. I had never stood up in front of the class before, but it looked so simple. All I had to do was read my paper out loud in front of my friends.

Denise, the girl sitting next to me, was terrified. She was shaking like a little puppy, and she was about to cry. I remember thinking how ridiculous she was to be frightened. I felt very superior to her because I wasn't scared. Then it was my turn. I strolled up to the front of the class, looked out over the room, and lost my voice. When I finally started to read, the words that came out were squeaky and odd. My heart pounded furiously, and my lips trembled so much that I could barely form the words.

Finally I sat down and fought tears while the rest of the reports were given. I was crushed. I had no idea how scared I'd be. I had been so cocky, and I felt that I had been hit with the ultimate put-down. Later I realized that this was an example of the old proverb, "Don't judge another Indian until you have walked in his moccasins." Much later, I realized this was what Christ meant by "judge not."

I remember this incident so clearly because today something similar happened. When I was a little girl, I believed that unless you were one of an unlucky minority, you automatically were born with two eyes, two arms, two legs, and two parents.

These were all part of the package of life, unless, of course, one of your parents had the misfortune to die. People who were divorced were in some way "different" and had some personal flaw that prohibited them from leading normal lives.

Then, when I was in high school, a few of my friends' parents divorced. While my attitude improved slightly, my convictions about divorcees were still colored by the narrow attitude of my childhood. I figured that people got divorced because their spouse was either a person unbearable to live with (grouchy, weird, or insane), or a lascivious adulterer. I believed that only Terrible People did such terrible things as divorce their partners. Of course, I felt sorry for the victims of the situation, the children of the marriage and the (undoubtedly) innocent and injured parent. Then I would think about how fortunate I was that neither of my parents had such awful or embarrassing problems; and how safe I felt knowing that a divorce could never happen in my family.

Well, now—six weeks after my parents have divorced—I have run into Scotty, one of my high-school friends, on campus. Scotty is handsome, brilliant, darling, and comes from the Perfect Family.

We were chatting on the sidewalk, and he asked offhandedly how my parents were. I had to tell him that they had divorced. I followed his reaction closely. He was genuinely shocked at first (although I think the shock was mainly because he hadn't already heard the news). Then a patronizing look spread across his face, and he said, "But I thought they were Christians. I used to see your family at church all the time." Then: "Oh, I feel so sorry for you," in an undertaker's tone of voice. That did it.

I was so mad I wanted to kick his shins, but I also didn't trust myself to say anything to him because I was afraid I would start sobbing uncontrollably and really give him something to be shocked at and feel sorry for. Here was a classic case of my own narrow perspective staring me in the face . . . only now I was on the other side! All I could say to him was, "Well, that's the breaks. See you around."

For the next hour, I talked to him in my mind, telling him all the things I didn't have the nerve to tell him in person. He had no idea of the pain and trauma of a divorce.

I know that Christians have a responsibility to try harder than non-Christians. In a Christian marriage, partners are held accountable not just to each other but to Christ as well. Divorce for Christians is the very last option, to be resorted to *if and only if* things get so bad that it means the death (in an emotional sense) of one of the partners. How terrible the pain must be before a Christian couple seeks this route as a solution! Divorced Christians aren't moral vampires or evil beings; they are victims of pain and trauma unlike anything Scotty could probably imagine.

Still, it stung that he had so misjudged our situation. Yet, after I cooled down, I reminded myself that I, in turn, should not judge him in my anger and hurt. I should forgive his lack of understanding. My first inclination was to straighten him out, to let him know how wrong his ideas were. My second was to try to understand his position. (After all, I had been there myself, right?) This last part is hard to do.

***

I talked with Daddy on the telephone tonight. I have decided to spend the three weeks between school and my job with him. He wants Cissy to come then, too, but her school doesn't get out until later. I don't know what she's going to do about dividing up vacation time.

Daddy's having a hard time. His girl friend has apparently taken up with someone else, and he is experiencing extreme loneliness, as well as a financial decline—two things he never had expected to face when he acquired his new freedom. I am sorry he is unhappy. He's having to learn to adjust along with the rest of us. I think he thought it would be a lot more fun when he was on his own.

After I hung up, I became very depressed. Here was Daddy, the one who wanted out the most, and he was unhappy. Why, I asked myself, did this have to happen? Why, why, why? And who or what was really to blame? Was it Daddy's job? The time he spent away from home? Was it male menopause? Was it Mother's interest in needlepoint instead of in a new, exciting career? Was it that they'd grown in different directions? What had caused their separation? Whose fault was it?

I would feel so much better if I could pinpoint an answer, especially if I could find an explanation which blamed something outside the family. But it was more complex than that and had to do with both parents.

"Incompatibility" is such a vague, unsatisfying umbrella.

Cissy called me. She was crying. Her roommate, who is obviously jealous of Cissy's good grades, had hidden her American history notebook last night, the night before the test. Cissy was nearly frantic trying to find it. Finally, thirty minutes before lights out, it "showed up" in one of her roommate's drawers. Anyway, Cissy had taken the test this morning and felt that she had done poorly. She had returned to her room during lunch and called me while everyone was still eating. I think the notebook incident was the straw that broke the camel's back. Cissy has kept a lot of bitterness and sadness all bottled up inside of her for several weeks, and it all came out at once when she called.

She told me she felt that it was unfair that our family had to break up. Several of the kids at school also had divorced parents, but her roommate and a couple of her roommate's friends came from "normal" families, and they didn't understand anything she was going through. It just isn't fair, she said, that some people's parents can work out their problems, and some can't. She said she was afraid she was going to be marked for life.

When our parents first started talking about separation and divorce, Cissy thought most of the blame lay with Mother. She has always been close to Daddy, and she could see his point of view better. She thought Mother had closed herself off in her own little world and wasn't trying to keep the marriage alive anymore.

Now, though, she thinks that Daddy is just as much at fault. She thinks he has made a mess of his life, and in the process has made a mess of Mother's and ours as well. She thinks both parents acted irresponsibly.

I sensed in Cissy the same need I had to find reasons why the divorce had to happen. Cissy had at different times blamed each parent in turn, depending upon whose side she saw most clearly and who pulled strongest on the emotional strings at the moment. I told her to hang in there. It wasn't easy, but we had each other and we had Jesus Christ to turn to.

After I said that, there was silence on the other end of the line. Then she said, "I've been so miserable that I've even blamed God for what has happened." She added, "I know that He didn't do it, but there are times when I feel like He could have prevented it if He had wanted to."

I told her that I had gone through the same stage.

The hardest part was not fighting with God about what had happened, but saying, "Yes, this has happened. Help us to grow stronger because of it."

By the time we hung up, she had calmed down and felt better. It's hard to get through these problems by yourself, and I'm glad we are close and can talk about them.

※﹡☙﹡☙﹡☙﹡☙﹡※

When my uncle died of lung cancer, we all knew his cancer resulted from his having smoked two packs of cigarettes a day for many years. We could blame his death on the cigarettes. But when one of our neighbors died of leukemia in the prime of her life for no apparent reason, we all had a hard time coping with her death. Her children blamed God, blamed the doctors, blamed everything they could think of until they realized her death was no one's fault.

Divorce, I guess, is similar. Some people are divorced for more or less definite reasons: desertion of spouse, wife-beating, even homosexuality. Most divorces are more complex. There are too many subtle, hidden, and deep things going on that many times the couple itself isn't even aware of. Nobody's fault, everyone's fault. Who knows for sure?

I feel I am wasting a lot of energy trying to get to the bottom and find out whose fault the divorce was. It would be better if I spent the energy learning how to accept the divorce and cope with it.

Next week I have three finals and two papers due. Today was the last day of class. I came back from history and sat down on the edge of the bed, looking out the window. Suddenly I was awash with sadness. The strange thing about this sadness, though, was that, first of all, it came over me so suddenly and unexpectedly. Second, it was deeper, stronger than the twinge of sensation I used to call sadness. It ran through my blood, rather than pricking my skin.

When I was little, I thought I knew what sadness was: a puppy run over in the street, the movie *Shenandoah*, the boy next door who lost his finger in a lawnmower accident. In comparison to the downpour of sorrow I've lately been experiencing, these were light April showers. Ever since divorce split up my family, sadness has taken on a new dimension.

As I sat there on the bed, looking out the window I'd looked out all year, I thought, "I'll never look out this window again after I leave." Then I thought, "I'll never be a freshman again; I'll never have this particular set of circumstances again in my whole life." Now these thoughts by themselves wouldn't have made me sad—just a little wistful, maybe.

Then it hit me—"I'll never have my family back again. We will never be under the same roof again." That's what knocked me out. I sat there as the sun went down, painfully, almost morbidly aware of how fast life gets away from us and how sad are some of the things we must learn to live with.

I wasn't sad just for myself and my family. I was bone-sad for all the sadness in the world, for people whose lives come to nothing, for people who literally starve to death on the streets, for people who are totally alone and don't know how to love, for people who have suffered worse tragedies than I could ever know about. It was as if I were floating down a great underground river with universal tributaries.

I wish Jesus lived right here and now on this campus. I would like to go and sit in His lap with His arms around me. And talk. And maybe cry.

Tomorrow I leave for summer vacation. Last Sunday, our college group at the church had a good-bye party. We were all wistful at the thought of parting for three months. I know I will miss their fellowship a great deal over the summer.

Chad and I said good-bye tonight. Daddy is coming to pick me up at eight in the morning, and Chad has his last final at that time. Chad promised to write and call me during the summer, but I will miss him very much. I don't know if I'm in love with him or not, but I know he has meant a great deal to me this past year. Saying good-bye was very sad, and I didn't sleep all night thinking about how much I will miss him.

V

SUMMER

Yesterday Daddy came to pick me up. We loaded my belongings in the car, and on the way out of town I asked him if we could go by Kathy's so I could tell her good-bye. I was a little embarrassed because we had awakened her, but I was glad we stopped by because she and Bruce are moving out to Oregon in a month.

After we left Kathy's, we stopped at the Howard Johnson's for breakfast and finally started driving after that. It was a long drive—it took practically all day. The bad part was that we ran out of things to say after about five hours. So we drove the rest of the way without saying much of anything and pulled into the garage of his new condominium about eight that night.

His condo is nice, but it doesn't smell like home, even though it is filled with familiar things. It feels like somebody else's house. Dad showed me the extra bedroom, which Cissy and I will share. It seemed like a hotel room which somebody had filled with mementoes and pictures from my child-hood.

I didn't sleep very well for the second night in a row.

This week has been strange. I feel like a displaced person. Dad has, of course, gotten up and gone to work every morning, and I have more or less sat around all day by myself. I don't know a soul except a guy whose parents live two condominiums down from Dad. He's asked me out twice and I've gone, but we really don't have much in common. I miss Chad. Every day I have taken my tennis racket down to the tennis courts to hit on the backboard in hopes of meeting somebody. So far all I've met are housewives and teenieboppers.

I've noticed one thing that has really changed since the divorce: our family rules. I don't just mean the understood list of dos and don'ts such as keeping our rooms straight, washing dishes three times a week, things like that, but also our family habits and traditions. For instance, we were always the first ones at our church on Sunday morning at nine. We sat in the same pew for years, and our family had belonged to the same church for genera-tions. Well, now Daddy has changed denomina-tions, and he goes to the five o'clock service. On top of that, he is always late! I can't get over this change. It's as if this ingrained tradition has been completely eradicated.

I remember Chad's talking about how, when the household is divided in two, all the rules, expressed and assumed, change. He said sometimes the divorce is so dramatic that the whole game is changed.

For instance: You thought all along that you were playing baseball. You knew who the pitcher was, you knew when it was your turn to bat, and you knew what happened when you struck three times at the ball and missed. Then, not only did they switch pitchers on you and move you from first base to short-stop, but they put a tennis racket in your hand and told you to make a field goal! It's suddenly crazy. No one has defined the game, much less a new set of rules. The whole field is in chaos.

That's the way I feel. I keep expecting things to bear at least a little resemblance to the way they used to be, but they don't. Instead of insisting on steak and potatoes the way he once did, Dad now eats only vegetables, rice, and fish—and that's all he talks about.

Another thing that Cissy had already discovered is our curfew. The rule at our house has always been that we could stay out in the evenings until eleven on week nights and midnight on the weekends, with exceptions for big parties and other special occasions. Mother is still holding to that rule. But Daddy lets both of us stay out as late as we want. In fact, Daddy often is gone himself until very late, at work or on a date, and he never knows what time either of us comes in. We have all the freedom we want. But this laxness in discipline is uncomfortable in a way. It's hard to switch back and forth. On the one hand, it's nice not to have restrictions, but in a way I feel as though he just doesn't care. Also, at Mother's I know what to expect.

***

Now that I'm about to leave to go to Mother's and start my job at the tennis clinic, I can look back on this three weeks a little more objectively. It's been a pleasant visit!

I have had the chance to know Daddy better than I ever knew him before. He was always so busy, or he kept to himself when we were around. Now, with just the two of us here, we got the chance to talk. As it turned out, we had more to talk about than at first I thought we would. Maybe in time I will learn to feel more comfortable when I visit him.

***

The first night I was at Mother's Chad called. It was wonderful to talk with him, but the way he found me was awkward. Mother and Daddy do not communicate any more. It's still tense between them, and they haven't gotten together since they were divorced. They only communicate by letter or telephone, and only about legal matters.

Chad had called my father's first and told him that he was trying to reach me. Something apparently had gone wrong with the phone at his dad's house, and he was having to use a pay telephone. So he left word for me to be by the telephone at a certain time when he could call back. Daddy had to call Mother's to give me this message, and Mother, of course, answered. Just talking to Daddy like that upset Mother, and I felt bad. Her conversation with him set off a whole string of questions about Daddy, and I had a hard time handling that. Being the go-between isn't easy, especially in such an emotional situation.

When Chad called back, we ended up talking for forty-five minutes. His father is almost his old self again, and Chad is picking up a course in business at the junior college in town.

I asked him how it was when his parents first divorced and he and Mark were the go-betweens. He said it wasn't easy. He felt that he was being used as a spy or a messenger. His mother, even though she was the one who left his dad, would ask him questions couched in polite and "innocent" curiosity, when actually she was pumping him. Questions like "How does your Dad like his new apartment?" or "I've heard his new girl friend has dated quite a few men. Is this true?" Chad said it didn't take much brains to figure out that she really wanted to know how Dad liked the new freedom he found in his bachelor pad and whether his new girl friend had loose morals.

He finally told his parents (because his father too would press him for information) that he didn't like being the go-between and that he felt awkward spying on each parent.

I asked him if he were going to spend any time at his mother's house during the summer. He said she had complained that he was not spending enough time with her, so he thought he'd spend the month of August there. He felt about her place the way I did about Daddy's. She had moved to a town where he knew no one, so he planned to take a number of books he'd been intending to read.

Anyway, it was good to talk to him. He told me he would keep praying for me.

***

I started working today at the tennis clinic. Roberta and I are teaching two beginning classes in the mornings and an intermediate class in the afternoon. I'm glad they assigned us to work as a team—we work well with each other. Roberta's boy friend Tommy also works at the clinic. He plays varsity tennis for the university and teaches advanced classes.

It feels good to be busy and useful again. It's also nice being around people I know, friends. The clinic has such a familiar atmosphere—I've been taking lessons here every summer since I was ten. I think

I'm going through a stage where I'm abnormally attached to any place that's familiar or part of my past.

Mother is making plans to look for a job this fall. She's spending the summer becoming, as she puts it, "de-traumatized." She's still flapping around like a bird with an injured wing.

I went with her to sign up for a course offered through the student union on how to get a job: how to write a resume, go through an interview, and all that. She doesn't have any idea what her job interests are, and she has a low opinion of her skills. For one thing, she's scared to death about having to support herself, and she resents the fact that, after devoting her life to raising a family, she is suddenly thrust out into the world to fend for herself.

I can sympathize with her. I can understand how scared she is. But at the bottom of her heart, she knows that God will take care of her. He always has in the past, and He always will. Even though she cries and feels frantic about the future, she is always able to turn around and put her life back into His hands.

I've noticed another way the family habits have changed since the divorce. This might have happened anyway, more gradually, as Cissy and I got older, but I've noticed that the roles have changed between parents and children. All our lives, Cissy and I have felt as though we needed our parents, that we were dependent on them. We needed them for basic things like food and clothes, but also for support, approval, and love. Even when we were going through our rebellious stages, I think we still needed their approval and love. But now, I feel that they need us, too, for support and approval and love—in a way that they didn't need us before.

For instance, Mother, as she is struggling with what she is going to do to support herself, keeps asking me for advice. She takes me into her confidence as she's never done before. I feel honored that she does, but I also feel a little helpless because I don't know quite how to respond or to help her. I just wish I knew what to say.

Yesterday I had the most wonderful surprise! It's the Fourth of July weekend, and I got a phone call from Janice, who was driving through town with her parents on their way to the coast for a vacation. I invited them to the apartment, and they stopped by for a Coke and a short visit.

Cissy had gone swimming, but Mother was there. I introduced Janice to her, and Janice introduced us to her parents. Janice is working at their church this summer, in the office, but she was able to take off a few extra days so she could go to the coast with her folks.

Janice's parents are as nice as I imagined they would be. Her mother is petite, and she has a gentle face and a warm nature. Her father is very tall, and I think "steadfast" would be a good word to describe the way he came across.

After they left, I felt so encouraged! It made me feel good to see a middle-aged couple who was still together and happy. It was obvious her parents still love each other, and Janice had told me one time last semester that her mother said their love grows stronger and stronger as the years go by.

Last night in my prayers, I thanked God for the example of Janice's parents. At a time when I was beginning to doubt whether anyone on this earth could have a Christian marriage for a lifetime, God has shown me that it is not an impossible dream. Marriage *can* work; people *can* grow in love and respect for each other through the years. Janice's parents are a good example of the kind of marriage that God had in mind for us when He said we were to become as one.

What hope! What encouragement!

Yesterday my favorite dress store had a half-price sale on all their spring and summer clothes. Mother and I went, because I need a new dress to wear to church and to start school in.

I hadn't been shopping with Mother in a long time. I walked behind her as we went flipping through the racks. It seemed that every dress she picked out for me I didn't like, and vice-versa. Finally, as my patience, and hers, wore thin, she took three dresses off the rack, laid them over my arm, and said, exasperated, "Here—go and try these on."

Well, I tried to be diplomatic about things. On the one hand I didn't want to hurt her feelings, but on the other hand, I wasn't about to get out of that store with a dress I didn't like. I told her I wasn't going to try those three dresses on; I didn't like them.

Things began to get tense. She wasn't used to my asserting myself like that. But at the same time, she's not unreasonable, and after I explained to her that I was nearly twenty and needed to choose my own clothes, she cooled down a bit. Then I cooled down, and we both started laughing.

We realized that we had not stopped to think but had moved back into a pattern from several years ago, when I didn't mind if she bought all my clothes for me. She decided to go over and look through the ladies' rack for herself, while I picked out something I liked. When I had selected two or three, I called her in for the final vote, and we both liked the dress I ended up with. As it turns out, she found a dress, too, and asked me for my opinion, which was flattering. So the afternoon worked out well, but there were a few minutes when I didn't know if we would end up driving home in stony silence or not.

Patsy, an old friend of mine from Sunday school, commented on my new dress today, and I told her the story of the dressing room. She had a story which tops mine.

Patsy and her mother were out shopping for a coffee table for Patsy's new apartment. Patsy and a friend had decided to move out of the dorm into an unfurnished apartment. For Patsy's birthday, her mother had given her the money to buy a coffee table; and she and Patsy had decided to go out shopping together to buy it. This little expedition took place between the time Patsy's father filed for divorce and the time the divorce was granted.

Problems started at the first store they walked into. Patsy's mother headed straight for the contemporary section, but Patsy wanted to look at the older, antique-type furniture. Patsy explained that she had grown up with her mother's chrome and glass and simple lines in furniture and had decided that it wasn't to her taste. She wanted each piece of her new apartment furniture to reflect her own style.

I could just imagine this, as Patsy was talking. Under the best circumstances, children and parents are going to knock heads when we try to establish our independence. I could see that Patsy's mom needed to let Patsy go, but at the same time she wanted to hang in there as long as possible to try to influence her daughter. And I could really identify with Patsy, needing to assert her own identity, but insecure about stepping out on her own.

Anyway, Patsy and her mother made it through

five furniture stores without having a blow-up. At the sixth, Patsy's mother found what she considered the perfect table for Patsy. When Patsy said, "No, thank you," her mother turned to her and said in a loud voice, "Well, Patsy, obviously you don't need me any more." She stuck a one-hundred-dollar bill in Patsy's hand and stalked out of the store.

Patsy chased her mother into the parking lot. Before she could catch her, she was already in the car and crying. Patsy, exasperated and embarrassed, tried to explain that she just wanted a wooden table, not a chrome one, while her mother kept saying that Patsy didn't love her because she didn't like her taste in furniture. The more they talked, the angrier they became. Finally Patsy stuffed the money back in her mother's purse, and said, "I don't want your dumb money," and walked home.

An hour and a half later when Patsy reached their house, she was able to apologize to her mother, and her mother to her. She told Patsy to go ahead and choose the table she wanted. But it took a couple of days before they were able to be comfortable with each other.

❖❖❖

Tonight I thought some more about Patsy. I decided this transition period, when we children are trying to break away from home without ripping everybody apart (including ourselves) is a rough time. I mean, it must be hard for parents to watch their babies grow up and flounder into independence.

But it's also hard for us as we try to break away. A lot of times we don't know what we want, but we know we want to find out *on our own.* We don't want to hurt our parents. We don't want to cut off all the home ties. But if we never leave the nest, we will be stunted human beings. There's no doubt about it—this is a tough time in any family; and it's especially turbulent and agonizing when the family itself is breaking apart.

We had a little mini-nightmare here this evening. Daddy called to speak with Cissy, and I answered the phone (which was fortunate). Cissy got on, and Daddy asked her if she had given his message to Mother yet. The message had to do with a sensitive question over a piece of land which Daddy bought about fifteen years ago. I don't understand it all, but the problem was about taxes on the land in the property settlement.

Cissy said she had given the message to Mother, but Mother had said she wasn't about to pay taxes on the land when the title was not in her name. Daddy became upset with Cissy because he said she had gotten the message all wrong.

About that time Mother found out that Daddy was on the phone. She started telling Cissy to tell Daddy what he could do with the taxes on the land. Poor Cissy was catching it from both sides. She told

Daddy that he'd better talk to Mother himself, but neither of the parents wanted to talk to the other one—they just kept yelling at each other through Cissy.

Finally Cissy got so upset she started screaming, threw the phone down on the chair, and ran out of the room. I had to get on and tell both of them at the same time that if they wanted this matter settled their lawyers or the tax man would have to handle it.

Cissy didn't calm down for about an hour. I went up and sat in the room with her until she stopped crying.

I remember Chad's telling me about one of his friends, Jeff, whose parents divorced when he was seventeen. Jeff's father had promised him a car when he was eighteen. But his dad had some pretty bad money problems at the time of the divorce, and Jeff knew better than to bring up the subject of a car for his birthday. In the meantime, Jeff's mother married a wealthy man. When Jeff's eighteenth birthday rolled around, his mother and stepfather sent him a gift certificate for the car of his choice.

At first Jeff was ecstatic. Then, shortly after he had opened the card, his father called, close to tears. He was even further in debt and was crushed that he couldn't buy Jeff a car for his birthday. He probably could afford one for Jeff's next birthday. Could Jeff wait just one more year? It had been his dream to provide his son with a car.

Well, as Chad said, Jeff was miserable. He knew that whatever decision he made—to accept his mother's and stepfather's offer, or to wait a year for his father's offer—he would hurt one or the other parent. His mother would take it as an insult to her and her new husband if he refused the car. On the other hand, Jeff knew his father would be devastated if Jeff let someone else, a stranger in Jeff's father's eyes, fulfill his dream as a father.

I can't remember what Chad said Jeff decided. All I remember is the terrible position Jeff was in, definitely a no-win situation all the way around. What's really sad to me is that both Jeff and his mom and dad had good intentions in what they wanted to do. Yet Jeff was forced to choose one parent over the other. I can't imagine being in that position if your parents are bitter and vindictive toward each other. But I am sure it happens every day.

The situation at our house was a little better this morning. Mother came into our room early and sat down and apologized to Cissy for last night. She said she realized that it isn't fair to put Cissy and me in that position but that she gets so mad at Daddy sometimes she just doesn't think. She said her behavior wasn't Christlike and asked us both to forgive her and to be patient with her when things like that happen. After she went back downstairs, Cissy and I decided we were lucky. A divorce could be much more painful and heal much more slowly if Christ weren't present in the people's lives. It's bad enough as it is, but at least we are all working toward a common goal.

I hope Daddy will write and apologize.

It's been raining for the last three days in a row, so we couldn't have our tennis classes. However, we were all required to hang around in case it cleared up, so we sat out under the covered patio and played spades and talked. I can't believe this summer is going by so quickly. A couple more weeks and I'll be going back to school. I wonder what's going to happen with Chad. He's been good about writing, but I wonder if he's changed. I wonder if I've changed!

One thing that's saved me this summer has been friends to talk with. I have realized that whatever our family has gone through, we are not the first nor the only people to have experienced a divorce. Just when I think that nobody else could have gone through such craziness or such pain, I hear about someone who has had a worse deal than mine. I think Christ gives us each other for help through the bad times.

Roberta told me of a good book to read called *Creative Divorce*. The chapter about children she especially recommends. It tells about the games that parents and children get caught up in during the struggle for emotional survival. Roberta said she could see how her family situation fit into at least two of the games.

Roberta's dad had been a hotel executive for twenty-three years, a stable, conservative, middle-class nice guy. He divorced her mother at the end of Roberta's junior year in high school. About a year later, when the divorce was finally settled, he let his hair grow, unbuttoned his shirt to the waist, wore medallions around his neck, and started taking out girls not much older than Roberta. During this transformation Roberta started college, and she never criticized him about his new life. However, when he suggested one time that he and Roberta double date, she put her foot down and told him, "Look—how you act is your business, but you're my father, not a buddy, and this sort of stuff embarrasses me."

While Roberta's father was playing "Pals," her mother was playing "At Least We've Got Each Other." Roberta had stayed in town to go to college; throughout the divorce and its aftermath, her sympathies lay with her mother. Her father had just walked out one day, leaving her stunned mother alone after a hysterectomy, and with a mare's nest of legal problems that took nearly a year to work out. Because Roberta's mother felt so abandoned, she leaned heavily on Roberta for companionship, knowing her daughter sympathized with her.

Roberta says that one of the main reasons she didn't go away to school was because she didn't want to leave her mother. However, before Roberta realized it, she was trapped at her mother's house, cooking supper five or six nights a week. Sometimes she turned down dates so her mother wouldn't be lonely. But when her mother started crying because Roberta had met Tommy and accepted a date two nights in a row, Roberta stopped and thought seriously about what was going on in the relationship. She decided the arrangement was stifling both of them. Her mother needed to find a life of her own and become more active with her own friends, and Roberta needed freedom to have her own social life, too.

So they talked about it, prayed about it, and decided that Roberta would move into the dorm second semester. Although Roberta still spent time with her mother, both were able to branch out and develop other friends and activities. This summer Roberta moved back in temporarily with her mother, but it's no problem. She and Tommy are able to go out when they want to, because Roberta's mom has gotten involved in other things and doesn't depend on her daughter the way she used to.

Next Monday I leave. Cissy's school starts the week after, but the dorms will be open early, and some of Cissy's friends will be there early too. Mother is going to drive us both up at the same time.

I got a letter from my new roommate, Monica Stevens. She's from New Orleans, and she sounds very nice. She's an education major, and she has four older brothers and sisters. I'm getting excited about going back to school.

VI

READJUSTMENTS

We registered for classes today. I have declared art education as my major. I had to have something to fill in the blank where it said "major," and I think that's at least close to what I want to do. I have debated between art and advertising, but I'll get more electives with art, and I have always wanted to be a teacher.

Monica is nice. She's also smart, and I think she'll be lots of fun to room with. Her parents brought her up to school with one sister and one brother, who are also in school here. I think her father is well-to-do, because he has three children in college and none of them had a summer job. I enjoyed meeting her parents. It was refreshing to see that some middle-aged couples are happily married and getting along just fine. It also made me sad for my own parents and a little envious of Monica.

My philosophy professor started off the first class by asking us to define "truth." As we each gave our various definitions, we began to see that even the definition of "truth" is larger and more complex than any one person's idea of it. He said he wanted us to realize early that the best we can do to understand truth is to pool our resources and come up with a conglomerate truth which, no matter how accurate or complex, never quite coincides with the greater truth existing outside our sensory understanding of a given situation. He told a story to illustrate.

Four women stood on a street corner after eating lunch together. Three talked together while waiting to cross the street; and the fourth, who planned to drive the others home, dug around in her purse for the car keys. One of the three was a woman about forty-two years old who had never been married and who had been badly hurt by several men in an unfortunate succession of unhappy love affairs. Another was her cousin, whose ex-husband was an alcoholic. The third was a woman who had a successful career as a doctor, but who fought constantly against the stereotype of the helpless female. The fourth, rummaging through her purse, was a housewife and content with her husband and three children.

As these four women prepared to cross the street, a collision occurred in the center of the intersection. A white Buick, driven by a forty-five-year-old man, slammed into the door of a green Pinto driven by a thirty-five-year-old woman who had been trying to turn left. The noise of the crash startled each of the ladies on the corner, who stood staring toward the center of the intersection. By chance, the police were within earshot and appeared on the scene seconds after the crash occurred.

No one was hurt. The two drivers climbed out of their cars and were soon in the middle of a fracas. The man swung his arms, wildly gesticulating and calling the woman names. She sobbed into a Kleenex. Each blamed the other. He claimed she had been trying to turn after the light had changed; and she claimed that she had already been in the middle of the intersection and that he had run the red light. In the meantime, the police found two empty beer cans on the floor of the man's car.

Because the four ladies were the only witnesses, the police pulled each one aside separately and asked her to explain the situation as she had seen it.

The woman who had never been married said, "We were standing here waiting for the light to change, and I noticed that the white car was coming awfully fast toward the intersection. I think the collision was entirely the man's fault, due to careless driving. He should have slowed down when he saw the light turn yellow; instead he sped up, probably exceeding the speed limit. And look at him now, the way he's treating that poor woman. No, it's entirely his fault."

The woman whose ex-husband was an alcoholic said, "The man is obviously drunk. He was speeding and out of control, and we should all be grateful he didn't kill somebody. I suggest you lock him up and suspend his license."

The doctor said, "The woman shouldn't have been trying to turn after the light changed. It's dangerous to sit in the middle of an intersection as she did, and she wasn't paying attention to the total situation. Now she should be standing up for herself instead of blubbering into her handkerchief."

The housewife declined to answer. She reported that she had her nose in her purse, and she didn't see anything until after the accident had occurred.

The professor asked us: What really happened? Did we think we could be more accurate than these ladies if we were standing on the street corner? He said that the law would find an answer. If the judge is fair and the facts are presented as accurately as possible, the judgment may reflect the truth, although law is not always a clear mirror of the truth. Regardless of what anybody said, the events of the collision occurred in a specific order and at specific times. (This could have been revealed by video tapes made of the accident.) However, the only record of the "truth" of the situation had to be provided by witnesses and people involved, all of whom had specific biases and perspectives which colored their interpretations.

That philosophy class has started me thinking. I've noticed that it's true—even if you're scrupulously honest, sometimes it's hard to find out what *really* happened. Even in our family, when we try to recall an incident that took place in the past, sometimes we come out with four different versions.

Since our family broke up, this memory business has been especially tricky, and the "truth" in various situations has become increasingly slippery. It's not because anyone is lying. No, all of us—both parents and Cissy and I—are quite sincere. As truly committed Christians, I think we are all expressing the truth as we see it.

As time goes by, however, to hear each of the parents talk, it sounds less and less like the same divorce. The "facts" remembered have become increasingly more distorted, depending on who is talking.

For instance, Mother tells how Daddy, in the early days of their marriage, never took her out to eat. They always had to eat at home, she says. But Daddy says that, up until Cissy and I were in high school, he took us all out to eat twice a week without fail. Cissy and I take a middle-of-the-road stand. We are convinced we remember going out to eat occasionally, but not necessarily twice a week.

What's so astonishing is that each of us is totally committed to the truth of his or her own point of view.

Chad and I have a religion class together this semester. It's fun to sit next to him in class, and already the class has sparked several ideas for us to talk about.

Seeing him again was even better than I had imagined. I had forgotten how tall he is and how handsome. He seemed glad that we were back together at school again, too. He told me he had cut out one of our party pictures and carried it in his wallet all summer.

Chad has started going with me to the Sunday evening group at the church. I'm delighted, of course. It makes an already special occasion even more special.

Janice had a good summer. She really enjoyed her job at the church. It was good to see her again and fun to introduce Chad to her.

-»§❊❊§«-

My philosophy class has a lecture twice a week in the auditorium, and once a week it divides into discussion sections, each headed by a graduate assistant. We'd been discussing different theories of reality, and at the end of the hour our graduate assistant asked us informally if we had any personal examples in which two people's versions of reality clashed. Several people talked about interesting things they had observed or that had happened to them, but the one I want to note here had to do with a classmate's parents, who'd been divorced for five years.

He and his dad met for lunch one day when his father was in town on business. They were having a pleasant visit, when his father looked up from his seafood gumbo and told his son with a perfectly straight face that he thought his mother (the father's ex-wife) needed psychiatric care because she didn't want to join him and the children for the Christmas holidays. He couldn't see why she would prefer her sister's company to a "family Christmas" like the good old days.

The student said he almost fell off his chair, but he tried to explain gently to his dad how hurt his mother had been five years ago when his father had run off with a twenty-three-year-old law student; how she had worked hard in therapy learning how to cope on her own; how she had gone back to school and now was leading her own life. He asked his dad to be realistic about his mother's position.

"Reality," said his father, "is that we were married for twenty-one years, and it's time we had a family Christmas like we used to."

Although his son told him that reality was quite different for his ex-wife, the father insisted that she needed to go back to the therapist to get straightened out. And that was the end of the discussion as far as he was concerned.

I've noticed a trap that children in a divorce can fall into. Because Cissy and I usually stand somewhere in the middle between our parents' versions, it's easy to think we see things the "right" way. I have to stop and remember that my lens is not clear, but tinted just like everyone else's. Also, my view of the truth in an emotionally-charged situation relates directly to where my sympathies lie. If I'm on Mother's side in one issue, sometimes I'll agree with her on something else before I've really stopped to think it out for myself.

It's all very confusing. It seems that we all live in one small area of a large jigsaw puzzle. All we can see are the pieces around us, never the total picture. God alone has the omniscient view. Our natures force us to wear blinders; we can never achieve complete understanding of things that go on in our lives. We have to trust that God will somehow bring all the pieces together.

❧❀❀❧

I'm really depressed.

Daddy has broken his leg, and they can't set it right. The doctors think he will never be able to walk without a limp. On top of that, Mother has finally started looking for a job, and she's been rejected three times so far in interviews. She's more down than I have ever seen her.

I wish I had the faith of Job, but I am really mad that God is sending down all these things on us. Why? I keep asking. Why? Just when we are getting over the first humps. Haven't we all had enough to go through?

❧❀❀❧

The sermon this morning was on grief. The minister told us the stages of grief—shock, denial, anger, self-pity, and, finally, acceptance. I was sitting there during the whole sermon relating these stages of grief to divorce.

Grief! I don't know why I had never considered what I was going through as grief before. But all the stages are there—the shock, the denial, the anger, the self-pity, and the acceptance. I've certainly run the gamut of these feelings, several times in fact, and sometimes I feel several of them all at once. I guess I'm grieving for the death of our family.

I see some difference, though, between grieving for the death of somebody you love and grieving after a divorce. If Cissy died, for instance, I would grieve for the loss of her presence in my life. I would know that she has gone home, that she is with Christ; but even though I could rejoice in that part, I'd still miss her because she'd no longer be here. I'd think about how much I loved her, remembering her mannerisms, quirks, habits, and the way she cheers me up. I might even remember how it drives me crazy when she twists the hair above her right ear.

But when you grieve after your parents divorce, there is nobody to grieve for, nobody whose presence is no longer in your life. Everybody is still alive and kicking. It's harder to grieve for an abstraction like "the family" because there's nothing tangible to miss.

Also, in grieving over a death, the family members pull together in their suffering. They get closer, and they support and love each other through the trauma. In a divorce, you also feel a need to pull together as a family. *But there's no family.* You end up grieving for the very thing you need but can't have. Knowing that you can never again have the support of the family makes the grief more intense.

After class today Chad took me to lunch. I told him about the sermon on grief and how I thought that people grieved after a divorce, too. He agreed with what I told him and added that the grief process after a divorce is further confused by several more things.

First, he said, when you grieve after somebody's death, the memories of the past are what pull at you. These memories are static, frozen in time. In a divorce, past memories also make you sad, but in addition, the participants are active in the present in unfamiliar roles. He said it was hard for him to see in the same person the mother who took care of him when he was a sick little boy and the mother who pranced around town on the arm of all the eligibles, drinking a little too much at parties. He wanted to grieve for the old mother, but he couldn't really grieve because his mother was still alive.

Plus, he said, each member of the family is suffering differently. Grief for us as children is different from the grief our parents experience. He made me stop and think. We think *our* grief is complex! Not only are our parents losing their spouse/mate/

friend of twenty-five years, but one or the other is probably feeling simultaneous bitterness at being left alone, fear of the future, insecurity at being adrift, anger at the way he or she has been treated, and shame at having failed in making the marriage work. How do you help each other work through all the grief when everything is so mixed up?

Working through grief is like filling a large hole. You're given a shovel and several piles of dirt. Any way you look at it, filling the hole will take much time and effort. You have several alternatives. You can leave the hole gaping in your life, refusing to admit that life goes on without your loved one; you can make half-hearted attempts to fill it, prolonging the process indefinitely; you can refuse to acknowledge the hole until it swallows you up one day; or you can get to work, praying for the strength to lift the shovel, knowing that it will take time and God's love to fill the hole.

During grief we have a Comforter: The Holy Spirit is present any time there is grief work to be done, no matter what the reason. Very slowly, little by little, He works in our lives to heal even the deepest kind of sorrow and grief.

In thinking how upset I've been with God for not letting us all be healed and whole again, with no more problems, I guess the miracle is not that God takes away the misery or gives us a shortcut through the path of grief, but that He is present with us as we heal.

I don't see much of Monica. She studies in the
library instead of the dorm room, and she is with
her boy friend almost every night. I've enjoyed getting to know her, though, when we have the chance.

She was born and raised an Episcopalian. Her
attitude toward religion is similar to what mine
might have been if nothing in my life had rocked
the boat. For instance, she always went to Sunday
school and heard the Bible stories about Jesus, and
her parents always prayed before meals and at bedtime. As she grew older, she was confirmed with
the rest of her sixth grade class, and now she goes
to church regularly without giving much thought
to what it all means at a personal level. In other
words, she's bought the package and hasn't yet un-
wrapped it for herself, which is exactly where I was
before I was forced to examine my faith. I think
that having your parents divorce either can make
your faith stronger, or it can make you cynical.

Cissy told me recently that a big problem she had
when our parents separated lay in her expectations
of them. Because our parents were the ones who
taught us and talked to us about God and took us to
Sunday school, she subconsciously tended to think
of them as demigods, or as God's representatives in
our lives. In her mind, they had assumed Godlike
traits, and she had Godlike expectations of them.
When she discovered they weren't perfect, she was
crushed. For a while, Cissy questioned the authen-
ticity of everything they had taught us about God.

She came to realize, however, that the fault was

not necessarily theirs for letting us down, but hers for having superhuman expectations of them. She's gotten over her disappointment at discovering their humanity. I think it takes children a long time to realize that our parents have flaws, just as we do. However, the great thing is that God uses everybody for His glory. I look at it this way: King David, great as he was, would not have looked so wonderful from his son Absalom's point of view.

❧❧❧

The main problem I've had to deal with is reconciling what my parents said and what they did. My parents raised Cissy and me to believe that:

1. Christians do not divorce.
2. Divorce is sinful and wrong.
3. Divorce is not even an option when marital problems arise.

So how do I bridge the chasm between what they hammered into my head and what happened to them?

I've been worrying about this for some time. Why are Christian marriages susceptible to divorce like other marriages? They shouldn't be. Not only are we told by Jesus that divorce is almost always wrong, but a commitment to Christ gives a couple greater strength in times of trouble. Worldly love has a tendency to fade and die out in time, but Christ's love only gets deeper and stronger and reinforces our intimate relationships. Christ's love,

which He gives to us and which we share with
others in relationship with Him, is a cut above anything we know as earthly love.

So what happens in a Christian marriage?

Do Christian marriages fail because, although
Christ's love is perfect, the people involved are
weak and tempted human beings who fall short? Is
it because of the frailty of our human condition? Is
it because of sin?

I don't know. I'm not sure I'll ever understand.

Our parents have both specified that for Thanksgiving and Christmas they want to split up the holidays and not us. In other words, they would rather
be with both of us for one holiday rather than one
of us for both.

Since Daddy has planned to fly East (leg cast and
all, if necessary) to be with some of his relatives for
Christmas, Cissy and I decided to spend Thanksgiving with Daddy and Christmas with Mother. Fortunately, Mother likes that plan. She has been invited
to Thanksgiving dinner by the minister and his
wife. Now that everything is decided, it all sounds
simple. But what a nightmare it was trying to get
everybody to decide on what they wanted.

At one point, before the minister invited her over,
Mother changed her mind and decided she wanted
one of us home for Thanksgiving and one at Christmas, which would have ruined the whole original
scheme. Then Daddy's leg problem came up and he

was afraid he couldn't fly, so he said he wanted us both home at Christmas instead of Thanksgiving. After that phone call, I was so exasperated, I called Cissy and told her we were going to hock all our belongings and take off to Hawaii for the entire holiday season.

Monica, of course, doesn't understand any of this intricate, delicate arrangement-making process. To her it's quite simple—everybody goes home for both holidays. She's very nice, though. She invited me home with her for Thanksgiving.

Janice also asked me to come home with her for Thanksgiving. I thought seriously about it but decided I'd better be with Daddy and Cissy. I asked her for a rain check, though. I'm fortunate to have such a thoughtful friend.

❊❊❊❊

Chad has been corresponding with a hometown friend whose parents broke up this fall. (I think Chad should go into the ministry, he's such a good counselor.) Anyway, his friend Randy wrote him a letter not long ago, which he shared with me. I've copied part of it because I think it's important. It starts out: "When my parents first decided to split, I'd been thinking about what being a committed Christian meant. I was at the swinging door between staying a Sunday Methodist and becoming a truly committed person. I have to admit that my first reaction was disgust at the mess two Christians had made of what was supposed to be the

sacrament of marriage. It was especially hard
where my dad was concerned. He'd been the spiritual leader at our house; he read the Bible aloud to
us before bedtime, he'd taught the high school Sunday school class at church for years, and he'd been
on the administrative board several terms.

"Then, suddenly, at this stage in his life some
things changed. He wasn't kind to my mother anymore. He belittled her in front of us, then claimed
she 'didn't understand him' when she became de-
fensive. I caught him in deception a couple of
times, when he tried to justify himself. And my
mom became like an iceberg. She never smiled,
never showed any response to anything except to
sigh and call my father a jerk.

"Was this Christian love? Was this what Jesus
wanted us to be to each other? At first I said to
myself—see? This is an example of Christian
hypocrisy, just like non-Christians are so quick to
point out about many Christians. Right under my
own roof are people who say 'love' with their
mouths, but don't live it with their hearts and in
their lives.

"I went through this cynical stage until I realized
that my own cynicism was a form of non-love, that
I myself was one of those same people I was despis-
ing: one who professed Christianity (for I never
stopped going to church), but who didn't love in my
heart. I had set myself above my parents and in
turn had judged them, a sin equally as bad. I realized, too, that part of my reaction was disappointment. Because Dad has been, in my opinion, God's

representative in our house, I felt that God had let us all down when actually God hadn't let anybody down at all."

❦

Not to love God and commit your life to Him because of the mistakes of two people (even if they're your parents) is, I think, a greater wrong than whatever it is they are doing to each other. I'm convinced that faith in Jesus Christ is the only way anybody can make it through a family's divorce. If we let Him, God in His infinite mercy, can use evil for good in our lives.

❦

We had a tornado here on the outskirts of town this afternoon—millions of dollars' worth of damage and nine people killed. The father of one of the girls who lives down the hall was out near his barn when the tornado whipped through his property and the barn roof came off and killed him. Her family is understandably distraught.

When I hear about things like this happening, I find myself asking the age-old question, *Why?* Why did it have to happen? Why to this particular family? I have the feeling I had when my parents first separated . . . has God abandoned everyone to his misery?

I have yet to come to terms with why there is pain in the world; why God, if He is all powerful, would allow such a thing in His creation.

When I was twelve, my face was burned in a car wreck. This was the first time that I had experienced real pain. I also experienced the pain of having people stare at me in public. But I healed quickly from the burn, and I had a good plastic surgeon. Relatively soon, I recovered from the whole ordeal.

When I was a sophomore in high school, a boy in my English class died. He was a fine Christian, a star on the baseball team, brilliant, full of potential, and he lay in unbearable pain for four months while a cancer ate his body from the inside out.

At the time he was dying, I went through the predictable reaction: anger at the apparent senselessness and waste. Why did such a fine person have to be taken? Why so young? Why such pain? Why was he given the gifts and the drive to develop them, then snatched away before his potential was realized?

Then, as I watched his faith grow stronger and stronger, I thought maybe God was using him as an example to show those around him what real faith is. Toward the end, I thought maybe God was going to perform a miracle. If everybody only prayed hard enough, he would get well. But when my friend only became worse, and finally died, I felt as if God had ignored our prayers. I concluded, therefore, that praying about serious matters was ineffectual. Finally I stopped trying to figure out why God would allow something like this to happen. I couldn't find any answers, so I shelved it and went on about my business.

I don't know how I can go on without coming to terms with why there is pain in the world. When I wake up in the night, miserable to the core about my family; when I watch Mother struggle to fend for herself, only to be rejected; when I think about Daddy, the operations on his leg and all the pain he's going through, it's no good to say, "Tough cookies, that's life." I have to find out: Is there any meaning to pain?

·❋❋❋·

Cissy and I rode the express bus to Daddy's for the Thanksgiving holidays. We got permission to miss classes on Wednesday; otherwise, it would have taken us all day Thanksgiving just to get there. Daddy picked us up at the station; he's rigged up his car so he can drive with his right leg in a cast.

Oddly enough, this Thanksgiving wasn't as depressing as last Thanksgiving was. Daddy was in a good mood in spite of his leg. He had bought a smoked turkey for us, and Thursday morning he spent several hours in the kitchen on crutches making what he considered his two specialities, wild rice with raisins and sunflower seeds, and a fresh vegetable salad. It was not a traditional Thanksgiving day dinner, but it was nice. We had some of his business friends over for the meal. Cissy and I thought it was interesting to meet some of the people he works with. All in all, it was an enjoyable holiday. There were a few wistful moments, and several times I thought about Mother; but it wasn't the doleful time I had expected.

On Saturday we were all sitting around, and Daddy was talking about his leg. He said that it felt much better—the main problem now was not the pain, but the itching inside the cast. So I asked him why he thought we had to have pain, pain of any kind, either physical or emotional.

He said he'd done a lot of thinking about that this year and decided that in spite of the fact that everybody tries to avoid pain, pain has some useful functions. If he hadn't continued to feel pain after they set his leg, he wouldn't have known they needed to reset it; and it wouldn't have healed correctly. So pain for him was like a warning signal that something was still wrong. He could name many people whose lives have been saved by the warning signals of pain. He said that lepers die, not because their bodies rot away, but because they have no pain sensors and therefore are unable to tell when something harmful or fatal is happening to their bodies.

I think the same is true, about pain being a warning signal, in an emotional sense. If you just ignore the little stabs and small painful comments made by a friend or a spouse, they can lead to great rifts and ultimately to the death of the relationship.

The next thing he said I didn't want to hear. He said that suffering strengthens faith and character. It sounded like an echo of what Mother had always chirped when something unpleasant happened to Cissy and me: "It will build your character." I wondered if Daddy were having to find this out first-hand right now, just as Cissy and I were.

Although I hate to admit it, it's true. Great pain can be the catalyst for spiritual and personal growth. Why grow—growing takes energy—when you are content and complacent? I have discovered a basic fact about myself: I have to be prodded to stretch and reach for a higher level of intimacy with Christ and a greater understanding of His truths. Without the painful wilderness periods in my life, I would be perfectly content going my merry way.

Cissy and I rode the bus back on Sunday. I tried to study on the way. I've got to buckle down in the next three weeks before we get off for Christmas. I've got two papers due, one in philosophy and one in my education class; and finals in religion, art history, and English.

I guess I'm going to have to ditch the idea that pain is an aberration of life, something which strikes you:

1. at random
2. as a result of a specific action or thought displeasing to God
3. because you are a bad person and deserve it
4. because God is trying to tell you something.

Apparently pain is an integral part of the fabric of life. Because of advertising and modern science I think we all grow up believing that life ought to be painless. For instance, we have elaborate and instant cures for both physical and emotional pain—drugs to cover everything from headaches to amputations plus scores of psychological and psychiatric clinics and counselors with all the answers for our emotional comfort.

I guess I'd better learn to accept it: Because we live in a fallen world, because sin exists here on earth, we suffer. I don't think God punishes us with pain; it's our fault that we have to live with sin, not His. After all, who ate the apple? The wonderful thing about Christianity is that God, in His grace, has redeemed us from sin, has saved us from having to live forever with pain. But in the meantime, here on earth, we suffer. Pain is part of life, and nobody—not even Christians—are free from it.

Pain, then, is one of the conditions of living, like being hungry at regular intervals. Well, I guess I don't feel so singled out for my particular kind of suffering. Nobody, when it's all said and done, goes through life unscathed.

※❀❀❀※

Chad and I went to hear a guest minister preach at the Methodist church this Sunday. His topic was unanswered prayers, and he said many good things. One thing in particular fit in with what I've been working through.

The minister started talking about prayers, how often we don't think prayers are answered because we are praying for what we want, not for what God wills. He spoke specifically concerning prayers for the alleviation or avoidance of pain. (I thought about our family's prayers, which had seemed to fly like white birds disappearing into the sky.)

Then he came to the point: Jesus, too, prayed for the avoidance of pain. In the Garden of Gethsemane, He said, "O my Father, if it be possible, let this cup pass from me . . ." (Matt. 26:39). While the minister continued his sermon along different lines, I pondered the implications of what he'd said. It suddenly hit me with a new force.

Jesus Christ, besides being fully God, is also fully human. Like the rest of us, He experienced human emotions, including pain. He knows its dimensions and depth. He knows what it feels like to have your friends let you down, to deny they even know you. He knows how it feels to be betrayed, to have mobs of people turn against you, spit on you, sentence you to death. I can't think of a worse way to die than on the cross. Not only was He totally exposed to the world in His agony; but the process of death, the ripping of His flesh and organs, must have been excruciating. Jesus *knows* suffering.

So then comes the overwhelming truth. Why did He allow Himself to go through this? For us. He knew how terrible the pain would be; but because there was no other way to atone for our sins, Jesus went through the deepest humiliation and a horrible death. In this way He fulfilled the second part of His prayer for the avoidance of pain: "... Nevertheless, not as I will, but as thou wilt" (Matt. 26:39).

I have finished my finals. All my papers are in. Tomorrow Cissy and I go home for the holidays. Last night Chad and I exchanged gifts because he had to leave this morning.

I have mixed emotions about going back for the holidays. Until last year, Christmas was my favorite time. I loved all the carols and the festivities. This year, though, I feel as if I've lost an old friend.

I heard a broadcaster say on the radio today: "According to research, more suicides take place over the Christmas holidays than during any other time of the year. The Christmas season, traditionally a happy time, can be the most melancholy time of the year for many people." Two years ago I would have flipped the channel, thinking, "How absurd—Christmas is great, even if you're not a Christian." But this year, I'm hoping that "melancholy" won't be an understatement.

Mother picked us up at the station and took us back to her apartment. We walked in expecting to see all our decorations up, but the only thing she had hung was a wreath on the door. No tree, no greenery. Oh yes, she did have the Nativity scene set up above the fireplace. She said that if we wanted a tree, we could go and pick one out. She had been too depressed to get one and decorate it by herself.

So the next morning Cissy and I walked to the grocery store around the corner and picked out a small tree, the best of the picked-over selection, and took it home. Then we got out all our tradition-al decorations and quietly put them on the tree. The low point came when we found a little Sty-rofoam angel that Cissy had made in nursery school, and Daddy wasn't here to make his usual comment, "Look how fat she is . . . been dipping in the cookie dough." We wanted to finish in a hurry, so we threw the icycles on in globs, something we had never ever done before.

Christmas Eve we went out to a cafeteria. Mother had not even unpacked the Christmas dishes. Then we went to the midnight service, where all three of us sniffled through the singing.

The next morning, we got up and exchanged gifts. Afterwards, Cissy and I volunteered to scram-ble some eggs. We sat around the table until noon, talking.

Christmas night we pulled ourselves up by our bootstraps and went out to see a movie. On the way home, we decided unanimously that the old meaning of Christmas with all its familiar, childhood associations needed to be boxed up and stored in the past. We would never have another Christmas like the old ones.

At first we were devastated with this sudden void. No one said a word for a long time. Then we all realized what had been staring us in the face all day. What was Christmas anyway? A time for parties? A time for presents? A time when you have to do the same things you've done for years and years? No. Christmas is Jesus' birthday. This was the essence of Christmas, which had gotten shuffled somewhere in the background: the celebration of Jesus' birth, the wonderful news that God was born into the world so we might have everlasting life.

When we stopped crying long enough to realize this, the profundity of God's gift to us in His Son made everything else about Christmas seem small.

Well, it's been nearly a year since the parents split up, and we've all made it through. Sometimes I've wondered if we would, but with God's grace we did. What will next year bring? Who knows—but it has a bright beginning. Daddy gets his cast off in mid-January, and it looks like Mother is going to get a job she wants, working in a travel agency.

VII

RESOLUTION

Mother drove Cissy and me back to school. We dropped Cissy by her school first and went in to help her unpack. Her roommate wasn't there yet, but a friend who lives down the hall had just arrived. We left them talking on the bed.

At my dorm, Monica wasn't back yet either. Mother wanted to drive home before it got dark, so I told her good-bye. A few minutes after she left, the telephone rang. It was Chad, calling to welcome me back. We talked for a while, then he asked if I wanted to go with him to the college group at the church. I told him yes and hurried to unpack my suitcase before he came to pick me up.

When we walked into the meeting, one of the leaders was directing a song. We slipped in the back and sat down on the last row of chairs. During the song, Janice saw me out of the corner of her eye and waved. We sang a few more songs, then our speaker stood up. He was a teacher from the university's religion department who spoke about the ways that the Scriptures are meaningful for our lives today. He was excellent.

After he finished, we prayed, and then we broke up for informal chatting before the closing evening service in the sanctuary. Chad started talking with a friend of his, and Janice rushed up and hugged me. "It's so good to see you," she said. We talked about the vacation, and she told me that she had prayed for our family during that time. We made plans to get together later in the week for a longer visit.

The group moved into the church for a short vespers service. Chad and I walked in together. Going inside, he slipped a piece of folded paper into my hand. I looked up at him, puzzled. He whispered, "Read it," as we sat down together in the pew.

I said a short prayer and opened the paper. It was a note with a poem Chad had written. It said, "I remember the pain of our first Christmas. I wish I could have been with you. I wrote this for you on Christmas Day:

> *God is nice,*
> *God is good;*
> *God would hug you*
> *if He could.*
>
> *God's in heaven,*
> *we're on earth;*
> *so Jesus came*
> *for our rebirth.*

Pretty soon
we'll see His face;
His arms will wrap us
in His grace.

But down here
while your burden's luggin',
I guess I'll have to do
God's huggin'.

I looked up at Chad, who was praying next to me. I squeezed his hand, feeling that my heart would overflow.

Then I looked up through the dim light to the stained-glass window over the altar. It was a picture of Christ with His hands outstretched, and the radiant light shone from behind Him. It was then I knew that, yes, Christ does live here on earth; He lives in the lives of the people in His church. We reach out to each other, we touch each other, we love each other through the power of God's love for us.

It was then I realized, too, that in Christ I had finally found my home.

EPILOGUE

I have wondered if there are any compensations for the difficulties my family has gone through because of my parents' divorce. It is a hard question to consider without sounding either like a cynic or a Pollyanna.

Though I know that God, if we let Him, uses everything to work for good in our lives, I still wish that we all could have avoided the experience. If there were a way for God to give us depth, insight, and maturity through osmosis instead of experience, I would be for it. However, since we children have little control over our parents' decisions concerning divorce, the question is not "*Am* I going to be faced with this?" (that decision is made for us), but "*How* am I going to cope with these problems?"

My sisters and I realized one thing quickly: We could either face the experience, learn from it, grow from it, and increase our faith from it; or we could let it make our lives bitter and unhappy, never resolving our problems and repeating the mistakes of our parents.

LESSONS LEARNED

1. The most obvious compensation that comes to mind is in the area of the role models our parents provided for us. Although we do not have a model of a successful marriage to pattern ours after, *we do have an example of what didn't work.* If we are smart, we will look closely at our parents' breakup and examine closely what went wrong. Then we can learn from what happened to them and possibly avoid this heartbreak in our own lives.

For example, our parents may have married for the wrong reasons—for security, money, looks, for social reasons, or for other superficial things, rather than for love, trust, and respect. We may be able to see this and avoid falling into the same trap.

Or we may see that our parents stopped communicating at some point along the line. This vividly brings home how crucial good communication is to the health of a marriage. We do not have to pattern our lives after our parents. We can learn from their mistakes as well as from their wisdom.

2. A second compensation of this experience is the confrontation at an early age of *the complexity of human relationships.* This confrontation is, of course, not exclusive to a divorce situation; everyone, I think, becomes more and more aware of how complex life is as they grow older. The old forked

tree of morality, with one fork representing right and the other wrong, suddenly grows into a tree with a million branches. Situations in which the *pure* right and the *pure* wrong are represented disappear.

As a simple example, consider a young couple in a neighboring town who are getting divorced. It is widely thought that she is a spoiled little rich girl who couldn't be happy with her husband's salary. At one time, I probably would have agreed with this, knowing what I do about the girl. Now I think, how true is this? She is painted as the difficult one, he as the angel.

But there are always two sides to every story; and the relationship, no doubt, has been more complex than this. Perhaps he withheld things or affection from her. Although she may have belittled him by lording her background over him, perhaps he was lazy at his work or squandered their money. Perhaps many things went on in the hidden heart of their marriage.

Complexity makes for discomfort. If you can peg him as right and her as wrong, then you have resolved the issue. This also oversimplifies most of life and is unfair to the total understanding of a situation.

3. *I have become more sensitive to all the nuances of a relationship*, which by themselves don't seem like much but add up to create a complete picture. For example, consider Betty and Charles Key.

Betty loved to cook pastries. Not only did she enjoy the results, but it was a source of pride for her to be known as a good cook. However, Charles, at an early age, was put on a prescribed no-sweet diet for his health. For twenty years Betty never stopped cooking sweets, and Charles, who had no willpower, never escaped from a continual state of either temptation or dangerous indulgence.

In retaliation, Charles smoked cigars his whole life, even though Betty was allergic to cigar smoke.

Either of these actions alone was not a crucial factor in Betty and Charles' marriage. Yet the cumulative effects of these and other repeated habits made up the fabric of their daily lives. It seems that much of marriage depends on the happy resolution of these small habits of living and consideration for the needs of the other person.

4. *Different people have different ways of showing and needing love.* I used to think that the need for love was expressed and fulfilled in universal ways. This isn't so, by any means!

One young couple worked through a rough spot in their marriage by recognizing and talking about this very thing. Because of his upbringing, the man brought a preconception to his marriage that if a wife loves her husband, she will spend hours in the kitchen cooking for him. He considered this to be one of the primary demonstrations of love.

On the other hand, the woman, whose parents were divorced, had different preconceptions. Because her father had often had financial troubles and her mother had refused to go to work to help out the family, she thought that if you really love your husband you will pitch in and help out by getting a job. Although it wasn't necessary in this couple's marriage for the woman to work, she held a good job. Since the hours prevented her from cooking for her husband, you can imagine the misunderstandings. She thought she was showing her love for her husband by working, but instead of getting support from him, all she received was cold disinterest. This was, of course, because he thought she really didn't love him, since she wasn't cooking him dinner. However, they were able to discover these feelings about each other and work out their differences. Now she works half-time, and both of them enjoy her newfound culinary expertise.

It's like the old story of the man who worked on his feet all day and his wife, who had a sit-down job. At night, his legs hurt from the strain, and her back hurt. They loved each other, so each one wanted to help the other. Because the man's legs hurt, he gave his wife leg rubs, thinking this was the best thing; and conversely, she rubbed his back. Although they had the best intentions in the world, they never met each other's needs.

When I think about the complexity of human relations, it's astounding that anybody gets along with anybody else, much less that some marriages survive and flourish through the years.

5. *I have gained resilience.* Although I still cry when I'm hurt, I am much tougher than I used to be. It's easier to ride the bumps. I still don't like hard times (who does?), but I know firsthand that crises pass and things start looking up again. By having gone through something like this at a young

age, I don't have naive expectations of life. I know I won't be destroyed if a tragedy hits later on in middle age.

When I was in high school, life had always gone smoothly for me and for my family. Although in one sense I took this for granted, in another sense I knew that it couldn't last forever. I used to think—what if Something Terrible happens? Could I make it through? The specter of this unknown doom used to scare me, because I didn't know whether I would fall apart in a tragedy or whether I'd be strong. Well, now I know that I can make it through a tragedy; and I have more confidence to face what life hands me. One of the crucial reasons is my faith.

At first, when I felt like the world had fallen in on top of all of us, I was angry and frightened. I was not a strong Christian at the time, and I neither blamed God nor looked to Him for support. Later, after the dust had settled and I still found myself standing on rock bottom emotionally, I decided that I had nothing to lose by placing my faith in God. When I did, I felt for the first time that I wasn't alone in carrying the burden of sadness and confusion.

Of course, things went up and down, up and down, after that. To say that suddenly I was happy or that my problems were solved isn't true. But most important, through all the following ups and downs, I discovered that God never left my side. Now I consider myself lucky to have had my faith tested. Christ became real to me during the time of trouble, and He continues to be actively present in my life.

6. The last compensation I can think of is, *I learned to put (and keep) my faith first in God and second in people.* When you have people around you who love you, it's easy to place too much faith in them. But people are people, and no matter how much they love you, they can't take God's place as the foundation of our lives. Humans are fragile; we are mortal, and whether we intend to or not, we let each other down. Christ is the only one in whom we can place our ultimate trust, and our relationship with Him should come above even our earthly family relationships.

THE CHOICE

I saw a poster recently that caught my eye. It showed lemons falling from the sky and a little man smiling and working a strange-looking, home-made contraption which gathered the lemons in an enormous funnel at the top and produced lemonade out of a spigot at the bottom. The caption said, "When life gives you lemons . . . make lemonade."

What came to my mind when I first saw it was Milton's observation in *Paradise Lost*, a quote I had to memorize for a literature class: "The mind is its own place, and in itself can make a Heaven of Hell, a Hell of Heaven."

I have always been interested to watch how some people can take a set of difficult circumstances and make out of them a cheerful and happy life, and how other people repeatedly create misery in the middle of what should have been good fortune.

A striking example of this came from a sermon I heard on the topic of the Christian fighting spirit. A famous doctor once had to amputate the right arm of two men in the same day. About two years passed, and by chance he saw, in one week, both men for the first time since their respective operations.

The first man came to him and said, "Dr. Smith, you wouldn't believe how my life has been going since I lost my right arm. I've lost my job, I'm not married, I feel like an outcast in the world, and I'm utterly miserable."

The second man came to him and said, "Dr. Smith, you wouldn't believe how my life's been going since I lost my arm. I have a new and better job than I did before, I'm married and have a brand new baby boy, and I'm beginning to wonder why the Lord gave us two arms in the first place. One will suffice."

So the choice is ours. God won't guarantee that no lemons will fall into our lives, but He will always help us make lemonade.

MY MARRIAGE

When I was twenty-six, I moved back to Austin, Texas, where I had gone to junior high and high school, and where my mother lived. I had been through many struggles in the previous two years, and I wanted to return to a place where I could heal and live a quiet life.

After I'd been in Austin for eight months, my mother and I went to the symphony one evening and sat directly in front of one of my old high school friends, Stockton Williams. I hadn't seen him in ten years. It took us both until intermission to work up the courage to reintroduce ourselves; but after we did, we had a good visit.

Several weeks later, he called and asked me to dinner. Looking back on our first date, we both see how the hand of God was in it. The timing of the get-together was perfect for both of us; we felt comfortable with each other immediately; we were able to talk about many different subjects; we could laugh with each other; and, most importantly, we discovered early that we shared the thing that was most essential to each of us: our faith in Jesus Christ.

Eleven months after our "re-meeting" at the symphony, I married this very intelligent and handsome man. I know how extremely fortunate I am. Not only does Stockton embody the finest Christian virtues of love, kindness, and understanding, but he comes from a wonderful, close-knit family. He has a living example of his parents' vital relationship and wants the same thing for our marriage.

We were married in December, and in early January we moved into a house we had bought. We'd picked out an older place to renovate. The

first year of our marriage we painted and wallpa-
pered and put a lot of ourselves into making our
house a home. Now that we have at least a few
pieces of furniture in every room, we are happy
with the results—we feel that the house is a "nest"
for us, and we hope it is a welcome place for guests.
Of course, this is not to mention the fact that the
grass in our backyard has completely died; and in
spite of all our efforts, we can't get the holly leaves
to stay on the bushes! Nevertheless, we love our
new place.

One of the most unifying aspects of our marriage
is our involvement in our church, St. David's Episcopal. At St. David's we have a dynamic team of
ministers and an excited, growing congregation. It
is a large church which provides a smorgasbord of
activities for every age and interest group. We have
worship services of all kinds: large, intimate family, formal, informal, folk masses, healing services;
we have small groups (prayer groups, theological
and Bible study groups, interpersonal groups) that
allow people to get to know each other on personal
levels; we have many different guilds and organiza-
tions for men and women. In addition, we have
active lay leadership: lay speakers, Celebrations of
Faith, contributions to the *St. David's Messenger* by
lay members of the church, and a group of talented
musicians who have put the Eucharist to music
and published it. Through all these various activities flows a spirit of unity that reflects the deep
commitment of the church's members.

Among our other church activities, Stockton and

I are taking Bible courses on Wednesday nights, we teach the two-year-olds every other Sunday, and Stockton is a licensed Lay Reader. Many of our closest friends belong to St. David's, including several couples who get together once a month for potluck suppers in each others' homes. All in all, Stockton and I find St. David's a place both for warm fellowship and for prayerful worship.

I am presently attending classes at The Episcopal Theological Seminary of the Southwest, where I am beginning work toward a Master of Arts in Religion degree. I am very excited about this new step and am greatly enjoying the classes at the seminary.

In conclusion, I would have to say that God has blessed my life more than I ever dreamed possible when I was going through the desert period after my parents' divorce. He has done what I had thought would be impossible: He has healed my wounds, and given me the courage to love.